Marian Cox

cirencester
college
a beacon college

Othello

William Shakespeare

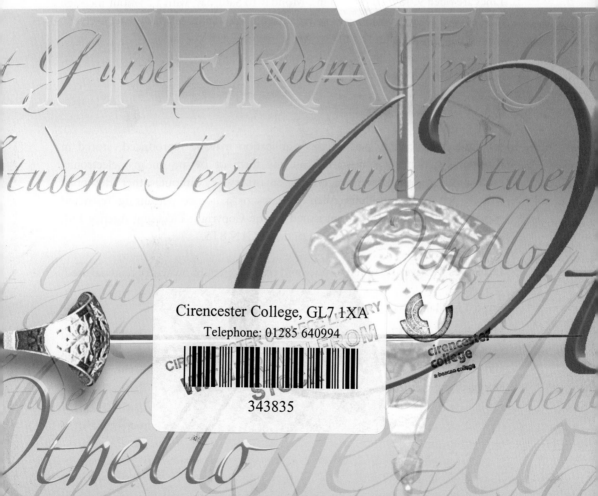

Philip Allan Updates, an imprint of Hodder Education, part of Hachette Livre UK, Market Place, Deddington, Oxfordshire OX15 0SE

Orders

Bookpoint Ltd, 130 Milton Park, Abingdon, Oxfordshire, OX14 4SB
tel: 01235 827720
fax: 01235 400454
e-mail: uk.orders@bookpoint.co.uk
Lines are open 9.00 a.m.–5.00 p.m., Monday to Saturday, with a 24-hour message answering service. You can also order through the Philip Allan Updates website: www.philipallan.co.uk

© Philip Allan Updates 2005

ISBN 978-0-86003-759-0

Printed in Malta

Hachette Livre UK's policy is to use papers that are natural, renewable and recyclable products and made from wood grown in sustainable forests. The logging and manufacturing processes are expected to conform to the environmental regulations of the country of origin.

Contents

Introduction

Aims of the guide

The purpose of this Student Text Guide to *Othello* is to enable you to organise your thoughts and responses to the play, to deepen your understanding of key features and aspects, and to help you to address the particular requirements of examination questions in order to obtain the best possible grade. It will also prove useful to those of you writing a coursework piece on the play by providing summaries, lists, analyses and references to help with the content and construction of the assignment. Line references in this guide refer to the *New Penguin Shakespeare* edition of the play.

The remainder of this *Introduction* consists of exam board Assessment Objectives and a revision scheme which gives a suggested programme for using the material in the guide. A section on writing examination essays gives practical advice on writing essay answers.

The *Text Guidance* section consists of a series of chapters which examine key aspects of the play including contexts, interpretations and controversies.

The final section, *Questions and Answers*, includes mark schemes, exemplar essay plans and samples of marked work.

Exam board specifications

Othello is currently a set text on four exam boards, two at AS and two at A2. It can also be chosen as a coursework text for OCR Unit 3 (provided that a different play is studied in Unit 1); the coursework must consist of two pieces (total 1,500–2,000 words). It can also be studied as the Shakespeare coursework text for AQA Specification B, Unit 3 (one or two pieces, total 1,500–2,000 words).

OCR	AS Unit 1	Closed book	Edition not specified
WJEC	AS Unit 1	Closed book	Arden, Penguin or Heinemann
AQA Spec A	A2 Unit 4	Closed book	Edition not specified
Edexcel	A2 Unit 5	Open book	Penguin Shakespeare

For **OCR AS** (closed book, 2 hours), candidates must answer two questions on *Othello*: a compulsory passage-based question in Section A, and a whole-text question (choice of two) in Section B.

For **WJEC AS** (closed book, 1 hour 30 mins) candidates must answer one two-part question on *Othello*, chosen from two alternatives. In each case the first part is passage-based, and the second part is a whole-text question.

For **AQA Specification A A2** (closed book, 2 hours), candidates must answer one question on *Othello*, chosen from two alternatives, in one hour.

For **Edexcel A2** (open book, 2 hours) candidates must answer one question on *Othello*, chosen from two alternatives, one based on a prescribed passage, the other on passages chosen by the candidate, in one hour.

Assessment Objectives

The Assessment Objectives for A-level English Literature are common to all boards:

AO1	communicate clearly the knowledge, understanding and insight appropriate to literary study, using appropriate terminology and accurate and coherent written expression
AO2i	respond with knowledge and understanding to literary texts of different types and periods
AO2ii	respond with knowledge and understanding to literary texts of different types and periods, exploring and commenting on relationships and comparisons between literary texts
AO3	show detailed understanding of the ways in which writers' choices of form, structure and language shape meanings
AO4	articulate independent opinions and judgements, informed by different interpretations of literary texts by other readers
AO5i	show understanding of the contexts in which literary texts are written and understood
AO5ii	evaluate the significance of cultural, historical and other contextual influences on literary texts and study

A summary and paraphrase of each Assessment Objective is given below and would be worth memorising:

AO1	clarity of written communication
AO2	informed personal response in relation to time and genre (literary context)
AO3	the creative literary process (context of writing)
AO4	critical and interpretative response (context of reading)
AO5	evaluation of influences (cultural context)

Othello has a total weighting of 30%, divided as follows:

OCR	AO1 – 5%; AO3 – 5%; AO4 – 10%; AO5i – 10%
WJEC	AO1 – 5%; AO3 – 5%; AO4 – 10%; AO5i – 10%
Edexcel	AO1 – 5%; AO2ii – 5%; AO3 – 5%; AO4 – 5%; AO5ii – 10%
AQA Spec A	AO1 – 6%; AO2ii – 5%; AO3 – 6%; AO4 – 7%; AO5ii – 6%

Note the different weighting of Assessment Objectives between the different examining boards for the same text. It is essential that you pay close attention to the AOs, and their weighting, for the board for which you are entered. These are what the examiner will be looking for, and you must address them *directly* and *specifically*, in addition to proving general familiarity with and understanding of the text, and being able to present an argument clearly, relevantly and convincingly.

Remember that the examiners are seeking above all else evidence of an *informed personal response* to the text. A revision guide such as this can help you to understand the text and to form your own opinions, and can suggest areas to think about it, but it cannot replace your own ideas and responses as an individual reader.

Revision advice

For the examined units it is possible that either brief or extensive revision will be necessary because the original study of the text took place some time previously. It is therefore useful to know how to go about revising and which tried and tested methods are considered the most successful for literature exams at all levels, from GCSE to degree finals.

There are no short-cuts to effective exam revision; the only one way to know a text extremely well, and to know your way around it in an exam, is to have done the necessary studying. If you use the following method, in six easy stages, for both open and closed book revision, you will not only revisit and reassess all your previous work on the text in a manageable way but be able to distil, organise and retain your knowledge. Don't try to do it all in one go: take regular breaks for refreshment and a change of scene.

(1) Between a month and a fortnight before the exam, depending on your schedule (a simple list of stages with dates displayed in your room, not a work of art!), you will need to reread the text, this time taking stock of all the underlinings and marginal annotations as well. As you read, collect onto sheets of A4 the essential ideas and quotations as you come across them. The acts of selecting key material and recording it as notes are natural ways of stimulating thought and aiding memory.

(2) Reread the highlighted areas and marginal annotations in your critical extracts and background handouts, and add anything useful from them to your list of notes

and quotations. Then reread your previous essays and the teacher's comments. As you look back through essays written earlier in the course, you should have the pleasant sensation of realising that you can now write much better on the text than you could then. You will also discover that much of your huge file of notes is redundant or repeated, and that you have changed your mind about some beliefs, so that the distillation process is not too daunting. Selecting what is important is the way to crystallise your knowledge and understanding.

(3) During the run-up to the exam you need to do lots of practice essay plans to help you identify any gaps in your knowledge and give you practice in planning in 5–8 minutes. Past paper titles for you to plan are provided in this guide, some of which can be done as full timed essays — and marked strictly according to exam criteria — which will show whether length and timing are problematic for you. If you have not seen a copy of a real exam paper before you take your first module, ask to see a past paper so that you are familiar with the layout and rubric.

(4) About a week before the exam, reduce your two or three sides of A4 notes to a double-sided postcard of very small dense writing. Collect a group of key words by once again selecting and condensing, and use abbreviations for quotations (first and last word), and character and place names (initials). (For the comparison unit your postcard will need to refer to key points, themes and quotations in both texts relevant to the specific theme or genre topic.) The act of choosing and writing out the short quotations will help you to focus on the essential issues, and to recall them quickly in the exam. Make sure that your selection covers the main themes and includes examples of symbolism, style, comments on character, examples of irony, point of view or other significant aspects of the text. Previous class discussion and essay writing will have indicated which quotations are useful for almost any title; pick those which can serve more than one purpose, for instance those which reveal character and theme, and are also an example of language. In this way a minimum number of quotations can have maximum application.

(5) You now have in a compact, accessible form all the material for any possible essay title. There are only half a dozen themes relevant to a literary text so if you have covered these you should not meet with any nasty surprises when you read the exam questions. You do not need to refer to your file of paperwork again, or even to the text. For the few days before the exam, you can read through your handy postcard whenever and wherever you get the opportunity. Each time you read it, which will only take a few minutes, you are reminding yourself of all the information you will be able to recall in the exam to adapt to the general title or to support an analysis of particular passages.

(6) A fresh, active mind works wonders, and information needs time to settle, so don't try to cram just before the exam. Relax the night before and get a good night's

sleep. Then you will be able to enter the exam room feeling the confidence of the well-prepared candidate.

Coursework

The coursework writing process differs from final examinations in being more leisurely and more supported by the discussion and drafting stages, but the issues of the play remain the same, as does the need for a relevant, focused response and references to 'different interpretations of the text by other readers'. A creative assignment 'must be accompanied by the candidate's critical commentary, explaining the rationale and the textual basis of the assignment'.

Coursework should be word-processed in the interests of presentation, consideration for the examiner, and ease of alteration for the student. There are a number of key stages in the coursework writing process:

- Once your title is decided and you are familiar with the Assessment Objectives, reread the play and all the notes and annotations you have made, extracting what is relevant for your title.
- With teacher guidance, read some background material and critical essays, and collect any relevant information from them. Keep a list of the books and articles you have consulted. Rephrase any ideas you borrow from elsewhere.
- Write a one-page essay plan, consisting of sub-headings and main points, and show it to your teacher to ensure you have covered the title fully and have adopted an appropriate essay structure.
- Write a draft of the essay, roughly the right length, based on your plan. Use details, examples and quotations from the text to support your points.
- Read through the draft, making sure that you have answered fully and remained focused on the question. Submit your draft to your teacher in good time.
- When your draft is returned, put into practice the comments offered to help you improve your essay and its grade, and adjust the length if necessary.
- Produce the final version, improving content, expression and accuracy where possible. Check the final word count. Include a bibliography listing the texts you have quoted from or consulted in the writing of your essay.
- After a final read through, putting yourself in the position of the reader, make last-minute adjustments and submit your essay — before the deadline.

Writing examination essays

Essay content

One of the key skills you are being asked to demonstrate at A-level is the ability to select and tailor your knowledge of the text and its background to the question set in the exam paper. In order to reach the highest levels, you need to avoid 'pre-packaged' essays which lack focus, relevance and coherence, and which simply contain everything you know about the text. Be ruthless in rejecting irrelevant material, after considering whether it can be made relevant by a change of emphasis. Aim to cover the whole question, not just part of it; your response needs to demonstrate breadth and depth, covering the full range of text elements: character, event, theme and language. Only half a dozen essay titles are possible for any set text, though they may be phrased in a variety of ways and they are likely to refer to the key themes of the text. Preparation of the text therefore involves extensive discussion and practice at manipulating these core themes so that there should be no surprises in the exam. An apparently new angle is more likely to be something familiar presented in an unfamiliar way and you should not panic or reject the choice of question because you think you know nothing about it.

Exam titles are open-ended in the sense that there is not an obvious right answer, and you would therefore be unwise to give a dismissive, extreme or entirely one-sided response. The question would not have been set if the answer were not debatable. An ability and willingness to see both sides is a high-level skill and shows independence of judgement as a reader. Do not be afraid to explore the issues and do not try to tie the text into one neat interpretation. If there is ambiguity it is likely to be deliberate on the part of the author and must be discussed; literary texts are complex and often paradoxical, and it would be a misreading of them to suggest that there is only one possible interpretation. You are not expected, however, to argue equally strongly or extensively for both sides of an argument, since personal opinion is an important factor. It is advisable to deal with the alternative view at the beginning of your response, and then construct your own view as the main part of the essay. This makes it less likely that you will appear to cancel out your own line of argument.

Choosing the right question

The first skill you must show when presented with the exam paper is the ability to choose the better, for you, of the two questions on your text where there is a choice. This is not to say you should always go for the same type of essay (whole-text or passage-based) and if the question is not one which you feel happy with for any reason, you should seriously consider the other, even if it is not the type you normally prefer. It is unlikely, but still possible, that a question contains a word you are not sure you know the meaning of, in which case it would be safer to choose the other one.

Do not be tempted to choose a question because of its similarity to one you have already done. Freshness and thinking on the spot usually produce a better product than attempted recall of a previous essay which may have received only a mediocre mark in the first place. The exam question is unlikely to have exactly the same focus and your response may seem 'off centre' as a result, as well as stale and perfunctory in expression. Essay questions fall into the following categories: close section analysis and relation to whole text; characterisation; setting and atmosphere; structure and effectiveness; genre; language and style; themes and issues. Remember, however, that themes are relevant to all essays and that analysis, not just description, is always required.

Once you have decided which exam question to attempt, follow the procedure below for whole-text and passage-based, open- and closed-book essays.

(1) Underline all the key words in the question and note how many parts the question has.

(2) Plan your answer, using aspects of the key words and parts of the question as sub-headings, in addition to themes. Aim for 10–12 ideas. Check that the Assessment Objectives are covered.

(3) Support your argument by selecting the best examples of characters, events, imagery and quotations to prove your points. Remove ideas for which you can find no evidence.

(4) Structure your answer by grouping and numbering your points in a logical progression. Identify the best general point to keep for the conclusion.

(5) Introduce your essay with a short paragraph setting the context and defining the key words in the question as broadly, but relevantly, as possible.

(6) Write the rest of the essay, following your structured plan but adding extra material if it occurs to you. Paragraph your writing and consider expression, especially sentence structure and vocabulary choices, as you write. Signal changes in the direction of your argument with paragraph openers such as 'Furthermore' and 'However'. Use plenty of short, integrated quotation and use the words of the text rather than your own where possible. Use technical terms appropriately, and write concisely and precisely, avoiding vagueness and ambiguity.

(7) Your conclusion should sound conclusive and make it clear that you have answered the question. It should be an overview of the question and the text, not a repetition or a summary of points already made.

(8) Cross out your plan with a neat diagonal line.

(9) Check your essay for content, style, clarity and accuracy. With neat crossings-out, correct errors of fact, spelling, grammar and punctuation. Improve expression if possible, and remove any repetition and irrelevance. Add clarification and missing evidence, if necessary, using omission marks or asterisks. Even at this stage good new material can be added.

Text Guidance

Contexts

The England of the early sixteen hundreds had just undergone a radical change of monarch and was involved in ambitious ventures of discovery and colonial expansion. The new century brought challenges to the Elizabethan world-view inherited from the Middle Ages, and this conflict is represented in the drama of the period. Below are some of the contemporary religious beliefs and social attitudes which throw light on the hopes, fears, thoughts and actions of the characters in *Othello*, and which Shakespeare exploits whilst simultaneously calling them into question.

Cultural context

The Elizabethans inherited from medieval theology the concept of a hierarchical **chain of being** on which every creature appeared in its ordained position on a ladder descending from God through angel, king, man and woman (in that order) to animal, vegetable and finally mineral. It is necessary to know about this belief in a divine order to appreciate the objection to women ruling men, and why it was believed that failure to apply reason reduced humans to the animal state of being governed by appetite and instinct. In Shakespeare a human who falls below the level of man into the realm of bestiality is labelled a monster. Many people thought at the time that moral sensibility was a product of social class, i.e. nobility of behaviour was a consequence of noble birth, and the word 'villain', used to insult Iago, comes from the Middle English word for peasant.

The ubiquitous presence of the word **Nature** in Elizabethan literature, in addition to imagery deriving from it and arguments about it, stems from the contemporary debate about the definition of Nature, which has two contradictory aspects: the benign and harmonious, and the malign and violent. Shakespeare's plays also examine closely the concept of human nature and its relationship to Nature as a whole.

External **appearance** was believed by many in Shakespeare's time to be an indicator of what lay within, i.e. goodness or evil. Appearance versus reality is a central issue in *Othello*, and the imagery of 'seeming' permeates the language of this and many other Shakespeare plays. If appearances, which are all we have to go on, are deceptive, and therefore character judgement is false, knowledge erroneous and truth elusive, then one cannot be sure of anything. This is the conundrum which torments many of Shakespeare's tragic heroes. Because Iago looks honest, Othello assumes him to be incapable of villainy.

Black was traditionally the colour of evil and of the devil, according to both Biblical and mythological sources. In Genesis God declared 'Let there be Light' to replace primeval darkness and bring truth and beauty into the world. An absence or putting out of light meant a descent into hell. 'Fair', 'white', and other words associated with light were part of a semantic field of beauty and goodness, whereas 'dark', 'dusky' and 'night' had the opposite connotations of ugliness and barbarism, which Iago is able to use to powerful effect against the sooty-bosomed Moor. A marriage between a black man and a white woman — and the idea of their possible 'filthy' progeny — would have been deeply shocking at the time.

The failure of **reason** was considered to be the cause of the Fall of Man (Adam allowed his love for Eve to overrule his better judgement and obedience to God), and Elizabethans therefore believed it was dangerous to let reason be dominated by passion. Characters in Shakespeare who become uncontrollably emotional are heading for a fall, as their intellect is what makes them human (superior to beasts) and keeps them sane. Othello gives way to his wrath and this is the downward turning point for him. In a state of heightened passion, such as anger and jealousy, mistakes are made, impulses are activated without sufficient reflection to moderate them, and one is no longer in control of oneself or of the situation.

Evil spirits were believed to be ever within ear-shot and on the watch for an opportunity to corrupt and snatch a human soul from the pathway of righteousness. Characters in Shakespeare who are foolish, **hubristic** or tempted enough to invoke spirits from murky hell to help them commit foul deeds are sealing their own damnation (as both Iago and Othello do at I.3.352 and III.3.444 respectively). One could also be tricked into carrying an evil creature, disguised as a fair one, across the threshold, with the same dire consequences. Othello fears this is what he has done in marrying Desdemona, and Brabantio in inviting Othello to his house. However, Othello's invitation to evil actually takes the form of giving ear to Iago's temptations and of bonding himself to him.

The fear of **damnation** and **hell** apparent in the works of Shakespeare and his fellow playwrights stems from a contemporary conviction that there literally was such a place below ground, inhabited by tormented souls allowed to walk the earth between midnight and dawn. Hell was typically portrayed the way Othello describes it, as engulfed in dark flames fuelled by sulphur (brimstone) to torture human flesh. The Elizabethans also believed in witches, diabolic possession and the incarnation of the devil and his agents in human form.

Telling lies was a form of deception considered to be a much more serious offence then than nowadays. It was a diabolical trick because Satan told lies to Eve in the Garden of Eden. Telling the truth was the way to shame the devil, and lying meant putting one's immortal soul at risk, especially since promises and oaths were thought to be witnessed by heaven. A gentleman's word was assumed to be the truth unless there was good reason to believe otherwise — which in Iago's case there is not — and it was a grave insult to call someone a liar.

Shakespeare had already dealt with **jealousy** in *Much Ado About Nothing* (1598), and did so again in *The Winter's Tale* (1610). Because irrational, jealousy was viewed as a sudden infection against which there was no prevention or cure. It eroded trust and dissolved the bonds holding together marriages, families and the social framework; it could let in the evil and chaos so greatly feared by Shakespeare's audiences. **Chaos** was the undoing of God's creation, a return to darkness and nothingness indicating the breakdown of the chain of being, the harmony of the universe, and nature's 'understood relations' (*Macbeth*). Shakespeare's contemporaries had a terror of a return of the anarchy of the civil wars period prior to the Tudor settlement and mostly peaceful reign of Elizabeth.

Romance was the genre of **courtly love**, represented in *Othello* by Cassio, the attractive ladies' man with his chivalrous manners and poetic language, devoted to the fair lady whom he worships as a divinity. She is expected to have rival suitors for her hand, competing for the right to serve her. Romance concerned exotic tales of magic, superstition and travel to distant parts, as well as love affairs, and brought together the masculine ideals of the soldier and the lover, as in the Arthurian legends. By definition the courtly lover had to be a member of high society and concerned above all with the notions of honour and reputation.

Cuckoldry, becoming a horned beast, was a prevalent male fear at the time, as it meant not only being an object of ridicule as a man who could not control his wife, and who had married a woman with unnatural sexual appetite, but was related to the wider issue of primogeniture and succession. Illegitimate children could not be assimilated comfortably into the family structure and were seen as a threat to the social fabric and the cause of inheritance complications and sibling resentments (as in *King Lear*). Though desirable, young and beautiful wives were considered dangerous as they were likely both to captivate their husbands and to be the target for seduction by other men, as Roderigo confirms.

The insistence on female **chastity** in so many Shakespeare plays is because the security of society and peace of mind of men was dependent upon women's virginity before marriage and chastity after it, meaning faithfulness to their husbands. In a society which passed inheritance down the male line, men needed to be sure that their son was really their own and not someone else's bastard, and a man's reputation would be destroyed by an unfaithful wife. Virginity and chastity were linked to religion via the Virgin Mary and regarded not only as an ideal state for women but as a test of the nobility of males, since only the higher orders were thought able to resist the temptations of the flesh, a claim Othello makes for himself to the Duke.

Historical context

The Venetian empire

While the remainder of Europe was ruled by monarchs and feudal lords, the northern part of Italy was unique in being organised into autonomous 'city-states'. Venice was one of the most celebrated of these; the first Doge (Duke) of Venice was elected in 727 and the Republic of Venice survived for more than 1,000 years. The republican Venetians elected a Grand Council composed of the most prominent citizens, which in turn elected the Doge. Shortly before the year 1000 AD Venice began to exploit its position at the head of the Adriatic Sea to found a sea-borne empire which would eventually stretch to the Levant and the shores of the Black Sea. The Venetian Republic fell into decline from 1570 onwards after the loss of Cyprus to the Turks. The position of Cyprus, at the crossroads of the eastern Mediterranean, helps to explain its history of invasion and subjugation over a period of 4,000 years.

The Turkish threat

The Christian world — Europe, north Africa, the Levant and Asia Minor — began to be threatened by Islam almost immediately after its creation in the seventh century. Moslems rapidly conquered all the non-European areas, and struck deep into Europe before they were defeated in France. The Christians launched a campaign to win back the holy places of Jerusalem from the Moslems in 1097 and achieved temporary successes. It was these Crusades which brought Europeans to Cyprus, which they colonised as an ideal base for operations in the Levant. The Ottoman Turks mounted increasingly powerful operations against the Christians from the fifteenth century, and in 1453 symbolically conquered Constantinople, the capital of the Byzantine empire. The remainder of Greece and most of the Balkans fell soon after, leaving Cyprus as a dangerously isolated Christian outpost in the Moslem world. The Turkish invasion of Cyprus of 1570–71, when *Othello* is set, consolidated Ottoman control of the region and they henceforth dominated the eastern Mediterranean.

Moors and Moslems

'Moor' and 'blackamoor' (a contraction of 'black as a Moor') were used very loosely in Elizabethan England to indicate any person of dark or black skin, including negroes, but correctly referred to those Moslems, originating in Morocco, who had conquered and settled in Spain from the seventh century AD. Parts of Spain remained Moslem and many Moors from north Africa settled there until the 'Moorish Kingdom' of Granada was finally defeated by the Christian Spanish Kings in 1492. The large Moorish population was initially allowed to retain its religion, but by 1526 Islam was outlawed and all Moors had been forcibly converted to Christianity as 'Moriscos'. Many fled the country both before and after this, and there were Christianised Moors throughout Europe by the end of the century. With his Spanish name and his 'sword of Spain', it seems probable that Othello was a Morisco expelled from Spain and hence a converted Christian. However, because England at this time was anti-Spanish, the English were anti-Morisco too.

There were two distinct ethnic groups involved in the Moslem conquest of Spain, and who hence came to be known as 'Moors'. The Berbers were the original inhabitants of the 'Barbary Coast', the Mediterranean shore of northwest Africa (the word Barbary is used three times in the play). They were conquered and converted to Islam by Arabs in the seventh century AD. The Berbers typically have much darker skins than Arabs, although not as dark as those of negroid Africans. Moors and Moriscos could be either Arabs or Berbers, and although it is uncertain which kind of Moor Shakespeare had in mind, the repeated references to blackness would hardly describe an Arab. In August 1600 the ambassador of the King of Barbary and his retinue visited London and caused a stir with their appearances in public over the next 6 months. A contemporary audience would have been familiar with Berbers, but much less so with negroes, and it is therefore likely that Othello is being depicted by Shakespeare as a dark-skinned Berber. Negroes and blackamoors were considered a problem in England in 1601, when it was decreed that too many had 'crept into the realm' and had become an 'annoyance'. Elizabeth I issued two edicts of deportation for their return to Barbary.

Black people at the time were represented either as savages and monsters, fit only to be slaves (see Caliban in *The Tempest*), or as mysterious and exotic chieftains. Whether menacing and repulsive heathens or romantic and heroic warriors, they were considered dangerous and unnatural because foreign. Thomas Rymer's interpretation of the play in the late seventeenth century as a condemnation of women who run away with blackamoors shows how a black general being permitted to elope with an upper-class white woman 'upset all contemporary notions of decorum'.

The four Moors in Shakespeare are, in chronological order, Aaron in *Titus Andronicus* (1593), the Prince of Morocco in *The Merchant of Venice* (1596), Othello (1602–03), and Caliban in *The Tempest* (1611), whose mother is from Algiers. All the plays refer to the fear of forcible miscegenation (cross-breeding); a child born to a mixed marriage in *Titus* is described as 'loathsome as a toad' (IV.2.67), a creature used in *Othello* to express disgust at the act of engendering. However, whereas Aaron and Morocco are stereotypically evil or undesirable characters, Othello — like Caliban — is much less definable. An 'other' is defined as someone who is somehow separated, stigmatised or noted as being different from the mainstream ideal. The literary stereotype of the alien has been much explored through the ages; in Shakespeare's time Jews and Moors fulfilled this role. Europe's response to the 'other' has traditionally been racism, misogyny and religious persecution, all of which are issues in *Othello*.

Theatrical context

Shakespeare and contemporary theatre

In the early seventeenth century, when Shakespeare wrote his major tragedies, drama had generally become more political, satirical, violent and tragic compared to the more lyrical tastes and pastoral works of the Elizabethans. There was a growing fashion for the use of artificial masque and elaborate spectacle in plays and poetry, and an emphasis on blood-thirsty revenge tragedies in urban settings among fellow playwrights such as Jonson and Webster. However, wit, irony and sophistication of ideas were still paramount in the plots, characterisation and language of the theatre. Play-going appealed to all sections of the population; the poor stood as 'groundlings' below the raised stage, whilst the wealthier sat in galleries or boxes. King James was a keen theatre-goer and supporter of Shakespeare's company, The King's Men, with a personal interest in witchcraft, religion and the role of the monarch. Contemporary playwrights catered for these tastes in their choice of subject matter and creation of characters.

Tragedy

Tragedy originated in Dionysiac choral song in the Greece of the fifth century BC. In tragedy, which involves disaster and multiple deaths, some undeserved, the events seem directed by fate, which ironically overrules the intentions and desires of the human victims, creating a sense of waste when exceptional people become fallen and their qualities are lost. The course which each tragic hero believes will lead to success in fact leads to destruction. Tragedies start with a serious early problem in the plot — related to death, war or failure of judgement — which develops into a catastrophic situation requiring further deaths and noble sacrifices in order for the previous status quo, with new participants, to be restored. During the drama there are 'incidents arousing pity and fear, wherewith to accomplish its catharsis of such emotions' (Aristotle, *The Poetics*). Tragedy (described as 'a painful mystery' by A. C. Bradley) has long been regarded as the highest genre of drama, having a philosophical seriousness requiring a playwright to produce work at the full stretch of his intellectual powers.

Shakespeare's tragedies

In Shakespeare the initial conflict is caused by a mistaken decision (usually the protagonist's), based on fear or desire, taken of his own free will and against advice or his own better judgement, which starts off a disastrous, irreversible and seemingly inevitable chain of cause and effect events as the hero falls from high to low. Evil or irresponsible acts committed by individuals spread to involve families, court communities and the nation, representing the contemporary belief in the connection between the **microcosm** and the **macrocosm**.

Whereas Time is the healing agent in comedies, it works against the protagonists in tragedy as coincidence and urgency, aspects of a malign fate. Act III is usually the climax of the conflict, and thereafter a sense of impending doom is created by the feeling that time is speeding up and out of control, until the **anagnorisis**, the hero's — and audience's — recognition of a painful truth about humanity and the universe. Because high tension cannot be sustained relentlessly for more than 2 hours in the theatre, there are quasi-comic scenes even in the most serious of Shakespeare's tragedies, which serve as ironic juxtapositions. After the multiple body count (at least five) and restoration of justice and order, a trusted character makes the final chorus-type speech summing up the tragic events and looking forward to a brighter future.

There are striking similarities between Shakespeare tragedies, particularly the four major ones written between 1601 and 1606, of which *Othello* was the second. The parallels lie not only in their plots, which are based on children and parents losing each other; siblings, friends or couples being divorced; murders by relatives; spying and lying. Characterisation, themes and imagery — such as words, appearances, monsters and poison — also echo each other across the plays; in addition they parallel and contradict each other, adding to the complexity. For instance, Iago is an inverted image of Hamlet as the amoral instead of the moral philosopher, one depending on demonstrable evidence and the other disregarding it. He is also, however, a parallel to the false Claudius in *Hamlet*, who can 'smile and smile, and be a villain'.

Nature is particularly important in the major tragedies, as a main source of imagery and the embodiment of paradox, being the origin of both health and disease, good and evil. In Shakespearean tragedy, uncertainty is of the essence, and fundamental human experiences and beliefs are questioned, with 'mighty opposites' being cross-examined but no verdict given. Along with the tortured heroes, we have to ask ourselves: What constitutes humanity? What are we here for? How can we tell right from wrong? Who is in control? We are asked for our moral awareness, but not our moral judgement, since no one is in a position to judge fellow humans or claim to understand the universe.

Shakespeare's tragic heroes

The tragic hero must be someone of eminent rank within his own society — a king, prince or military leader, someone 'better than we are' (Aristotle). In classical terms, they become guilty of **hubris**, an act of presumption as mere mortals; their over-reaching is punished by **Nemesis**, goddess of retribution, and the audience is expected to respond by feeling 'the pity of it'. The 'noble hero' makes what Aristotle called an 'error of judgement' (Greek *hamartia*), which traditionally has been translated as 'fatal (in both senses of the word) flaw'. The mistake is traceable to a character fault, and this, in unfortunate conjunction with circumstance and coincidence, causes the tragic hero's awesome fall 'from happiness to misery'. During his fall he will undergo ironic and sudden reversals which bring him up against the 'realization of the unthinkable' (Leech). The sense of waste and loss comes from the fact that the hero has superhuman qualities in other respects and could have gone on to achieve great things; or as Marlowe put it in the final chorus of *Doctor Faustus*: 'Cut is the branch that might have grown full straight.' Because free will is involved, an accident of birth or fate alone cannot be blamed, making the retribution more complex and a cause of concern to all humans.

Shakespeare's major tragic heroes appear to have little in common: Hamlet, the young intellectual Dane, treated as a difficult adolescent; Othello, the not-so-young general and blackamoor, newly wived; King Lear, widower of over 80 who loses his grip, his mind and his daughters; Macbeth, the married but childless Scottish warrior and serial killer. However, they are all driven mad in one way or another, and lose touch with their former selves. In each case women — whether wives, daughters, mothers or witches — are a force for an extreme of good or evil, or ambiguously both, and crucial to the development of the hero, the plot and the tragedy; they seem to represent nature and what it is capable of.

Shakespeare's heroes die ambiguously, either achieving a kind of dignity by showing courage in the final moments, even though possibly continuing to labour under a delusion, or passively cooperating with the workings of divine necessity. The classical view is that 'The tragic hero makes a fuss' (Leech) about what has happened to him and the injustice of the world, and dies fighting back rather than accepting the unacceptable. The other, Christian, view is that by recognising his error, taking responsibility for it, repenting of it and accepting punishment, redemption is possible for the hero. In either case tragic heroes express the hope that they will survive in the memory of their friends and the state, and that their true story will be told, with its mitigating circumstances, to reduce their culpability and to prove that death can be transcended by fond memory, historical record or legendary status.

Play context

It is widely assumed that Shakespeare never left England, though the majority of his plays in all genres are set in other countries; Italy was favoured particularly because it was the origin of the Renaissance and home to many of the source texts which inspired Shakespeare and his contemporaries. Foreign settings also have the advantage of allowing comments on local political and social issues to be made circumspectly, as in *The Tempest*. Shakespeare wrote two plays set in Venice, a city of interest to Londoners as a major trading rival to which English merchants travelled and brought back reports of its luxuries and vices. Exaggerated travellers' tales were in vogue at the time *Othello* was written. This is the only Shakespeare play to be set in roughly its own time, 1570.

Shakespeare used known sources for 35 of his 37 plays, and it is assumed that the other two must have had sources as yet undiscovered. In this period, before, and for some time after (until the emergence of the aptly named 'novel' genre in the early eighteenth century in fact), originality of plot or character was not considered necessary or even desirable in literary works; a largely illiterate population and a traditional oral culture created a demand for the reassuringly familiar. Audiences expected to know already the basic storylines, settings and outcomes of plays they attended, and the skill and creativity of the playwright was demonstrated by the quality of the improvements made to an existing work, including the adaption of the genre.

There is a particularly full and detailed source for *Othello*, namely Giraldi Cinthio's story — which may have been called 'El Capitano Moro' — in his collection of 100 tales called *Hecatommithi*, published in 1565 in Venice. There is not known to have been an English translation until 1753, so Shakespeare may have read it either in the original Italian or a French translation.

He may also have been influenced by a tale in Geoffrey Fenton's *Certaine Tragicall Discourses* (1567) in which a foreign soldier kills his innocent wife out of jealousy. There is also evidence that Shakespeare made use of Lewkenor's translation of Cardinal Contarini's *Commonwealth and Government of Venice* for information about the Venetian state, and of Philemon Holland's translation of Pliny's *Natural History* for the exotic details of Othello's career given in his speech of defence before the Venetian Senate.

Cinthio's story

Comparing Shakespeare's play with its source makes it possible to understand and appreciate *Othello* better. The list of statements below describing Cinthio's version gives the main differences between the short story and the play, and you should consider in each case why Shakespeare's version is an improvement.

- the only named character is Desdemona
- Othello is called only 'The Moor'
- there is no elopement
- there is no Turkish threat
- the couple travel on the same ship
- Iago falls in love with Desdemona
- Iago's sole motive is sexual jealousy of Cassio
- Iago has no hatred against Othello
- the murder plot is against Desdemona only
- there is no Roderigo
- Desdemona's father is not mentioned specifically
- Cassio does not suffer from drunkenness
- Iago has a young daughter
- Iago steals the handkerchief himself
- Cassio recognises the handkerchief
- Iago's wife knows the whole story
- Iago and Othello kill Desdemona together
- the murder is presented as an accident
- the Moor is killed by Desdemona's kinsmen
- Iago is tortured to death for another crime

The printed text

No manuscripts of any of Shakespeare's plays have survived. Some of the plays were published during his lifetime, in editions known as 'Quarto' from the size of the paper used. After his death, a collected edition known as the First Folio was published in 1623 which contains all his plays except *Pericles*. Although the Folio is generally considered to be more reliable than the Quartos, for each play the case has to be considered on its merits.

Othello was first published in Quarto in 1622, 6 years after Shakespeare's death and just a year before the Folio. There are nevertheless significant differences between the two texts. Any decent edition will have an appendix discussing the textual problem, in which the editor will explain and justify the choice of text. The *New Arden* edition (ed. E. A. J. Honigmann, 1999) is principally based on the Quarto; the *New Penguin* (ed. K. Muir, 1968) is based more on the Folio.

Although we cannot know with confidence the origins of the copies of the play, there are generally three possibilities: the author's rough draft, or 'foul papers'; a prompt copy prepared for use by a theatre; a fair copy made by the author. Whichever it was, the text was often copied by a scribe, and then typeset in fixed metal type by a compositor, and errors or changes could creep in at any stage of this process. The Folio text is 160 lines longer than the Quarto (mainly because it includes Desdemona's Willow Song and Emilia's 'double standards' speech). On the other hand, more than 50 instances of profanity printed in Quarto were deleted or replaced in the Folio, which is believed to be due to the Act of Abuses, passed in 1606, which prohibited swearing on stage. We know that Shakespeare often revised the texts of his plays, and made deletions, and there is no consensus as to which is the more genuine or reliable text. Since he rarely provided localities or stage directions, a lot has been left to the discretion of editors through the ages.

Whichever edition you use, a number of changes will have been made from the original text. Different editors often have different views and arrive at different conclusions. The changes, and arguments for them, are usually indicated in the textual notes, but generally, the goal of an editor is to produce an edition which makes sense when acted on the stage, rather than to give an account of all the possible interpretations of the play.

The Tragedy of Othello, The Moor of Venice

Othello (full title above) is one of the four great tragedies of the first decade of the seventeenth century and was probably written in 1602 (though a later date has also been argued) but in any case before its performance in 1604, and between *Hamlet* (1600) and *King Lear* (1605). Honigmann, the editor of the *Arden* edition, believes it was inspired by the visit of the ambassador of the King of Barbary to London in 1600–01, with his retinue known as 'the Barbarians', which was much discussed by Londoners at the time. Honigmann points out that also in 1600 a translation of John Leo's *A Geographical Historie of Africa* was published, in which Leo, a Moor brought up in Barbary, wrote about his fellow countrymen is terms very similar to the character traits of Othello, calling them 'honest', 'proud', 'high-minded', 'addicted unto wrath', 'credulous', 'subject unto jealousy', and willing to lose their lives rather than put up with disgrace on behalf of their women.

Othello has been called a tragedy of intrigue, as opposed to a tragedy of revenge, a popular type of play at the time, though the two are related. Jealousy and cuckoldry were traditionally topics for comedy, and there are scenes in the play, notably the harbour scene and the street scenes, which are typical of this genre. Many of the characters are also recognisable stereotypes from contemporary comedies, such as the gull (the fool, i.e. Roderigo), the senex (old man, i.e. Brabantio) and the clever, plotting slave (Iago). There is also a classic scene of comic cross-purposes (Cassio's supposed confession in Act IV scene 1) which can be compared to the scene in *Twelfth Night* when Antonio demands his purse from the wrong twin. The play employs two other comedy conventions: the 'calumniator [slanderer] believed' and the 'deceiver deceived'. What is daring about *Othello* is that comic devices enrich the tragedy by providing an alternative perspective on it, rather than by being juxtaposed with it, as in *Antony and Cleopatra*. In *Othello* the ludicrous and risible is an inseparable element of the tragedy, which makes it the more poignant and ironic.

The play on stage

First performed at court in the autumn of 1604, *Othello* has been in continual production for 400 years — with constantly changing attitudes towards it and inter-pretations of it — and was originally one of the most popular Shakespeare plays. However, notions of refinement, decency and female sensibility meant that from the Restoration to the recent past, performances of expurgated and abridged versions of the text were the norm, and this was particularly true in the eighteenth century, when the clown scenes, the character of Bianca, sexual language, Othello's fit, and violence against Desdemona were all omitted. The Willow Scene (Act IV scene 3) is usually drastically cut, and justified on the grounds that the song is omitted from the Quarto. Unjustifiable insertions have also been made to add to the tragic pathos, especially in the final scene.

More than any other Shakespeare play, *Othello* has caused controversy and audience reaction has been painfully intense. Unlike in *King Lear* and *Macbeth*, the killing of a woman takes place on stage, which creates a highly charged scene and a disturbing one for audiences. Spectators have frequently been driven to call out warnings and advice to Othello, or denunciations of Iago.

Race, costume and age are questions affecting the portrayal of Othello. Shakespeare knew that Moors could be tawny-skinned if they came from the Barbary coast of north Africa. Despite Roderigo's intended insult of 'thick lips', probably a racist exaggeration, it is likely that Othello is of a lighter skin colour than Negro-black. As a proud Christian, it is unlikely than Othello would be dressed differently from the Venetians, though the stage Moors of the plays performed in the 1590s, such as *The Spanish Moor's Tragedy*, wore turbans and carried scimitars to indicate religion and temperament. Two of Shakespeare's other Moors dress in this flamboyant and stereotypical way. Although Othello is supposed to be a lot older than Desdemona (at least 20 years and probably 25), many productions cast them as equals in age. Another question for the director/actor is whether Othello should have a foreign accent (representing in English his non-native use of Italian).

Though a relatively short play (average 205 minutes) it is very emotionally and physically demanding of the actor playing Othello, particularly during his seizure in Act IV scene 1. He has to manifest extreme behaviour and passion throughout the second half of the play, and it has been known for illness to result. There have been two kinds of Othello over the years: the dignified, lyrical and sensitive versus the passionate, sensual and violent. Richard Burbage, the leading actor in Shakespeare's company, first played the part of the Moor and his performance was considered deeply moving and acclaimed one of his greatest successes. Other notable Othellos over the centuries have been Thomas Betterton in the early eighteenth century; Edwin Booth, a refined and polished Moor in the nineteenth century; Tomaso Salvini, who made animal noises and movements, was tempestuous, spoke his lines in Italian and was the first Othello to strike Desdemona; Lawrence Olivier, who stressed his race and sexuality, and gave an 'outlandish vocal performance' (*Arden* introduction, p. 28).

Iago is on stage in nearly every scene and therefore he is under pressure and the scrutiny of the audience almost continuously. He must not look or behave like an obvious villain, or this would destroy his credibility and the point the play is making about the unrecognisability of evil. The crucial thing for an actor to get right is Iago's body language and facial expressions, and to find the balance between his being a damaged human and diabolically powerful. Actors complain that motivelessness is unactable, and that Shakespeare himself 'has not got a clear line on Iago'. It is interesting that so many famous actors through the centuries have tried their skill in the roles of both Othello and Iago, even switching alternate nights in some cases.

Desdemonas have to decide how passive to be in their delivery, tone and movements. For instance, does she stay in bed in Act V scene 2 or try to escape from her psychopathic husband when she realises his intent? Is she completely innocent and naïve, or does she deliberately put on a girlish and flirtatious act to get her own way? Minor characters also give scope for varying and even opposite interpretations. Roderigo, for instance, is usually played as a comic character fooled and mocked by Iago and held in contempt by the audience for his weakness and gullibility, but the Oliver Parker film portrays him as a dangerous and explosive character driven to more and more violent and desperate acts.

The tempo of the play is fast, sustained and tightly plotted, with many scenes starting *in medias res*. There is no redundancy, recapitulation, change of action focus or use of peripheral characters, as there are in the other major tragedies — particularly when directors omit, as they often do, the two short Clown scenes (III.1.3–29 and III.4.1–22). The audience, like Othello's and Desdemona's emotions and reputations, is subjected to continuous 'verbal mugging' (*Arden* introduction, p. 64). There is continuous tension from Act III onwards, to the extent that it is difficult to find a place for an interval; the only possible place, logically, is between Acts III and IV, but this destroys the dramatic intensity of Iago's verbal assault upon Othello and a break here is anti-climactic.

Critical history

Othello was the fifth most popular Shakespeare play — *Hamlet* being number one — in the seventeenth century. In 1692 however, after the Restoration, the play was attacked in the 'hysterical criticism' of the notorious Thomas Rymer for its improbability, its lack of justice, and its character assassination of common soldiers: the character of Iago was deemed incredible because soldiers are genuinely honest! It was also interpreted by Rymer, and others later, as a warning to maidens not to run away with blackamoors and to take better care of their linen.

If the reward for innocence is brutal death, then the play can be seen as immoral. This particularly bothered the first real generation of critics in the eighteenth century (who also caused the ending of *King Lear* to be rewritten so that Cordelia and Lear did not die), and Dr Johnson admitted to finding the final scene of *Othello* unendurable.

Shakespeare's genius and the achievement of the tragedies was not fully appreciated until the Romantic period, when analysis of psychological states and human relationships became the focus of critical interest. Coleridge was an influential critic who responded intuitively and sensitively to the emotions being explored through the medium of the main characters, and who coined the famous phrase concerning Iago's apparent 'motiveless malignity'. The play remained popular throughout the nineteenth century, with Iago's character as the centre of literary debate. In the first half of the twentieth, however, an argument was begun between A. C. Bradley and F. R. Leavis on the issue of Othello's nobility, the latter arguing against it. To the present day critics are divided over the extent to which they consider Othello is to blame, and over whether Othello redeems himself in any way at the end; T. S. Eliot thought not. Bradley found the play depressing, and Granville-Barker declared it a tragedy without meaning.

Domestic tragedy?

Though often present on exam specifications, *Othello* is the least popular of the four great tragedies because it is commonly deemed to be more domestic and less universal; it is shorter than the others and seen as narrower in scope and lacking profundity in its commentary on humanity. Unusually, there is no subplot or parallel plot in *Othello*, which intensifies its claustrophobic atmosphere, along with the relatively small group of characters. Tolstoy called the play 'the tragedy of the bedroom' to convey this microscopic focus, though at another level the play is on a grand geographic scale embracing a large part of the eastern Mediterranean. It may be true that we do not actually like or sympathise with Othello very much, partly because his adversary is the one with the humour. There may also be a suspicion, arising from his lack of perception, that Othello is not very intelligent or sensitive. A modern perspective may make it easier to identify with problems less related to theology and chastity than those which underpin Othello's dilemma.

Othello is, however, as much concerned with the **eternal verities** as the other three major tragedies, since it continues *Hamlet*'s preoccupation with the power of words and shares with all of them a study of relationships, of the nature of evil, and of the paradox of nature, preparing the way for the breakdown of family and social bonds in *King Lear*, and of 'understood relations' in the universe of *Macbeth*. In all of them there is the worrying impossibility of distinguishing appearance from reality, of telling 'the mind's construction in the face', of exercising judgement, and of verifying knowledge. In addition to these grand themes, *Othello* has poetry, power, pathos — and some of the most fascinating and controversial of Shakespeare's characters.

A variety of critiques

Any play must be considered in relation to its historical and social background and the political climate which produced it, and be viewed in the context of contemporary attitudes, however unconsciously drawn on. This is especially true of Shakespeare's only play set in his own time. On the other hand, our critical interpretations should include responses to the issues which concern us nowadays, such as the stereotyping of race and gender in the portrayal of women and black people. A feminist critique will try to ascertain whether the play challenges or accepts and endorses the patriarchal status quo and the misogyny of the time; a post-colonial critique will study the way Othello is portrayed as the 'other' in a white world; structuralist approaches will look at language to expose the shifting and ambivalent relationship between words and meaning (signifier and signified); post-structuralists will look for what isn't there as well as what is, at how the plot is framed and at the assumptions being made. A combination of all of these critical approaches will produce essays which show an awareness of a range of reader responses and audience reactions, and which cover the examination assessment criteria.

Scene summaries and notes

Act I scene 1

Roderigo and Iago are in the middle of an argument concerning Desdemona's secret marriage to Othello. Roderigo has been paying Iago to promote his own interests with Desdemona. Iago explains that he has been passed over as lieutenant to the Moor in favour of the inexperienced Cassio. He assures Roderigo that he hates Othello and only continues to serve him for his own ends. They wake up Brabantio to tell him his daughter has eloped with Othello. When he is finally convinced that the previously rejected suitor, Roderigo, is telling the truth, Brabantio orders an armed search to arrest Othello. In the meantime Iago has slipped away to warn Othello.

Othello's name is not used at all in this scene, although it is all about him, and the active anti-Othello party serves as a pattern for the rest of the play, whereby negatives dominate before positives have a chance to speak for themselves and the audience's mind is already poisoned. Othello is presented as the stereotypical lustful Moor. A 'gross revolt' from nature has occurred in Desdemona's choice of partner as far as all characters present are concerned, all of whom use racist language. Iago's first words are blasphemous, and Venice is presented as a place of corruption, conflict and disturbance. Monetary diction and the verb 'to know' are established in this opening scene, as is the battle between Christian and heathen. Iago shows himself in possession of a lot of knowledge about Othello's movements. Iago is in danger of losing his main source of income, his 'purse' Roderigo, by this marriage, and must therefore do something about it. The 'Lieutenancy' is a key issue as military rank and power were consonant with virility and attractiveness to women; Iago has been hit where it hurts by having both denied him and Othello and Cassio being considered superior in both love and war.

Other key words are introduced – service, honest, seeming, poison, devil – as well as farmyard animal images. The problem of Cassio's 'fair wife' (see V.1.19–20) has much exercised editors, one view being that it should read 'fair life'; the *Penguin* editor thinks Shakespeare must have changed his mind later and made Cassio unmarried but forgot to correct this line; the *Arden* editor gives three other suggestions, the most convincing being that Cassio is a womaniser and not fussy about whether his women are married or not. It could also mean what it says: Cassio has a beautiful wife, who is living in the Venetian garrison with him, and is therefore known to the lascivious and envious Iago, and Iago is expressing his belief that men who marry beautiful wives are damned because they will inevitably be cuckolded. Iago does not reveal himself to Brabantio, and this is the beginning of using others for his own ends while covering himself. Iago's statement, 'I am not what I am', ironically echoes God's words to Moses in Exodus: 'I am that I am'. The play starts in darkness, with a call for light at the end of the scene. The newly-weds are disturbed in a way which echoes the contemporary practice of *charivari* – noise made outside the couple's house on the wedding night to show disapproval of the marriage. Their elopement characterises them as romantic and dramatic; it could also be interpreted as the product of the 9-month gestation in the decadent womb of Venice.

Act I scene 2

Iago claims, doubly falsely, that he wanted to defend Othello against Brabantio's slanders but is not evil enough to commit murder. He tries to stir up enmity between Othello and his father-in-law, but Othello is confident that he can 'out-tongue his complaints' and he asserts his noble lineage. Cassio and the Duke's servants find Othello first and request his presence at the Senate, followed immediately by Brabantio's followers including Roderigo. Brabantio accuses Othello of having bewitched Desdemona. They all go to the Senate for Othello to answer the case against him.

At this stage Othello does not allow himself to be provoked by Iago, who is forced into the position of onlooker when the others arrive. The theme of division is introduced with the word 'divorce'. The theme of battle is enacted by two armies meeting in the street, one with the intention of fighting. Cassio is presumably lying when he tells Iago he knows nothing of the marriage, as he has been the go-between throughout the courtship. The final couplet in this scene summarises the fear and prejudice in Venice against Moors and barbarians, 'bondslaves and pagans', who threaten to reverse the natural order.

Act I scene 3

Brabantio publicly repeats his accusation of witchcraft against Othello, who responds by telling the story of their courtship, and how Desdemona was wooed by pity and fascination for his sufferings and exotic travels. When Desdemona arrives and is asked to verify his story, she chooses her husband over her father, and Brabantio disowns her, despite the Duke's plea for mercy. Because Desdemona is now an outcast, and because she wants to travel with Othello, they both beg the Duke to allow her to accompany Othello on his mission to Cyprus. It is agreed that Desdemona will follow the next morning under Iago's protection, and with his wife as her maid. Brabantio's last words are a threat to Othello that his daughter will deceive him too. When they are left alone, Roderigo threatens Iago that he will drown himself for the loss of Desdemona, but Iago quickly convinces him that if he accompanies the party to Cyprus, with plenty of money at his disposal, Desdemona will turn to him when she tires of the 'erring barbarian'. In his soliloquy, Iago reveals his suspicion that Othello may have slept with his wife, and his plan to get the lieutenancy by making Othello think Cassio is having an affair with Desdemona.

The stream of messengers to the Duke demonstrates the urgency of the crisis and indispensability of the 'valiant Moor'. The confusions, doubts and contradictions of the messages also show the impossibility of distinguishing truth from the deception of 'false gaze'. 'Error', 'judgement', 'reason', 'proof' and 'test' are words used by the Duke, which prefigure Othello's situation later. Othello's speeches to the Senate reveal the 'Othello music': rhetorical devices, poetic imagery, strong rhythms and the characteristics of varnished tales. The question of whether he is deliberately self-dramatising or using high-flown language unconsciously influences our response to him as a character, and divides the critics. This is in any case a trial scene, with Othello as the eloquent defendant and Brabantio as the aggrieved prosecutor. Brabantio's description of his daughter as hitherto a 'maiden never bold' suggests either that he has never really known her, or that Othello/love has caused a complete character change, since she took the initiative in the love affair. She has overcome the fear of Othello's outward appearance by seeing his 'visage in his mind', testifying to the power of imagination. Her accompanying him on such an expedition to a war zone was extraordinary for a wife at this time. There is the possibility that Desdemona has behaved unnaturally, and that the basis of the relationship is the somewhat flimsy one of a shared romantic idealism and Desdemona's capacity for pity. Conversely, the scene can convey a devotedness, trust and compatibility between the beleaguered couple.

Mention of monsters and cannibals is relevant to various themes, as is the idea that words, tales and fictions can form a captivating web and evoke overwhelming emotion. Othello and his wife must say farewell to peace and Venice, home and father; division has entered their lives and 'haste', 'speed' and 'time' must be obeyed; love has been subjugated to a call to arms, Iago's run of luck has begun and death is being mentioned already.

Contempt for women and noble virtues, including love, and a habit of comparing humans to animals is evident in Iago's manipulation of Roderigo, the stereotypical unrequited lover. Like other Machiavels, Iago makes it clear he believes in free will, not destiny, and that life is what you make it. His speech (lines 331–67) contains ten injunctions to Roderigo to put money in his purse, but Roderigo is unaware of this effective technique of subliminal brainwashing. One of Roderigo's roles is to make Iago reveal his theories and practices so that the audience can be impressed by his cunning strategies, and prepared for his later conquests.

The theme of reputation is evident in this scene and is a concern of all the characters in it. It is composed of blank verse, couplets and prose, each change signifying a change of mood and dramatic effect. The structure is paralleled in many other scenes, i.e. private conversation becoming public debate and ending with a soliloquy by Iago. This gives the impression that Iago is controlling events on all levels, that he is the only character who can connect the public and the private, and that he is omnipresent. A notable feature of the play is how all domestic moments are hijacked and turned into performances or trial scenes, and that Desdemona and Othello are not permitted to have the privacy of a married couple. The final couplet contains images of conception, evil, light and dark, and Iago summons 'all the tribe of hell', i.e. invokes evil spirits. Critics have noted the way Iago's use of 'And' in line 381 gives away the lack of specific motivation for his hatred of Othello and makes the adulterous allegation seem unconvincing.

Act II scene 1

Cassio arrives in Cyprus first, then Iago and Desdemona, and finally Othello. They have been held up by a terrible storm which destroyed the Turkish fleet. Cassio provokes Iago when he courteously kisses Emilia and puts Iago down as being only a soldier and not a scholar. Iago persuades Roderigo that Cassio must be 'displanted' as he stands in the way of Roderigo's chances of Desdemona turning to him when she inevitably tires of the Moor. Iago's soliloquy states his plan to avenge himself on both Othello and Cassio, whom he also claims to suspect of having cuckolded him.

Storms are used in Shakespeare, and literature through the ages, to represent disruption to normality and as a portent of disaster. The division of Othello from his wife and his lieutenant because of the elements presages the emotional divisions soon to follow. The external Turkish threat is replaced by that of the Turk within Iago, which is harder to deal with because invisible. Anxiety and tension is created by the delayed and staged arrivals and the fear of Othello's demise. Dramatic arrivals and the uncertainty of identity are continuing features from Act I. Ironically but fittingly, the salvo to announce Othello's arrival is mistakenly given for Iago instead, who has had 'most favourable and happy speed'; he has overtaken Othello, whose ship left many hours before his, and has arrived a week earlier than could have been expected, as if favoured by the gods. Cassio offers a 'Hail Mary' to the 'divine Desdemona', uttering hyperbolic flattery of a traditional courtly kind. She indulges in banter with Iago to hide her anxiety about Othello's safety, thus being guilty of putting on an act. Her apparent flirtation with Cassio confirms Iago's claim to Roderigo that he is her 'second choice' and therefore must be removed. Wearing his clown's mask, Iago unfairly criticises his wife for talking too much and gives vent to his misogyny, calling women 'wild-cats, devils'. The theme of speech, tongue, words, slander is further reinforced here, and 'Alas, she has no speech' previews Desdemona's and Emilia's end. Iago's aside to the audience forces us to see others the way he sees them, i.e. naïve and foolish, and we are impressed by his powers of improvisation. His description of Cassio as 'a slipper and subtle knave, a finder out of occasions' and 'a devilish knave' applies to himself and indicates how Iago sees everyone in his own image.

Act II scene 2

A herald declares that Othello has granted an evening of celebration for the destruction of the Turkish fleet and for his own marriage.

It is ominous that these two events of war and love have been linked, and in that order.

Act II scene 3

Cassio is put in charge of the watch while Othello and Desdemona retire. Iago tricks Cassio into drinking to the point of drunkenness and Roderigo provokes him according to plan, immediately confirming Iago's slanderous prediction of Cassio's uncontrolled behaviour to the governor, Montano. Cassio strikes Roderigo and wounds Montano, who has intervened to stop the fight. Othello is roused from bed and to anger. He dismisses Cassio from his service after hearing Iago's cunning account of the incident. Cassio appeals for advice to Iago, regretting the loss of his reputation and denouncing the demon drink. The latter plays the good friend and tells him to use Desdemona to try to get his place back since the 'General's wife is now the General'. Roderigo is again persuaded to continue the chase and to trust Iago.

It seems clear that we are meant to understand, despite critics who argue that it never happens, that the marriage is consummated at the beginning of this scene, as Iago lewdly informs us. His description of Desdemona is low and coarse, contrasting with the flattering and courteous comments Cassio makes about her. Iago has set up revellers to trap Cassio into having to be sociable, and to drink the health of 'black Othello' or prove himself ill-mannered. Thus Iago uses virtues as well as faults against their owners to unmake what has been made: the lieutenancy, the marital union and the respect of Cypriots for Venetians. In Iago's view, real men can hold their drink, and be the life and soul of the party, as he can. Drunkenness was seen as a state akin to bestiality, since it involves loss of clear vision and reason and is an 'enemy in their mouths to steal away their brains'. Iago is also a kind of poison that can be called 'devil', and has the same effect. Iago's song reminds us of the theme of reputation/status and how it rankles him to be thought of 'low degree', aggravated by Cassio's claim that salvation is according to rank, and the 'Lieutenant is to be saved before the Ancient'.

Iago manages the action, entrances and exits, and timing of this scene in masterly fashion, and comes out of it well himself; he diminishes people's reputations, both in their own eyes and in the view of others, and raises himself in everyone's esteem. Luck takes his plan further, making Cassio wound Montano, the real cause of Othello's embarrassed annoyance with his lieutenant. The ringing of the bell is a warning of the enemy's advent, and is a symbolic alarm that the Venetians have 'turned Turks' and are behaving barbarously, thanks to Iago. Whenever Iago can get in a reference to sex, he does so, as in the 'bride and groom/Devesting them for bed', and his speech equates love with 'opposition bloody' and the battle imagery of 'swords', 'tilting', 'odds' and 'action'. Speech, and the disadvantage of those who can't speak (Cassio and Montano), is made clear in this scene. Double-talking Iago can speak in a way which both condemns Cassio and yet appears to be pleading on his behalf, as a loyal friend would. It is of crucial significance that Othello says 'My blood begins my safer guides to rule,/And passion, having my best judgement collied,/Assays to lead the way' (lines 199–201). This is tantamount to having fallen; letting passion overrule the safer guide of judgement was Adam's original sin. To reinforce a recurring image, 'collied' means 'blackened'. Othello never recovers from his giving way to the deadly sin of wrath at this moment.

The dismissal of Cassio without having heard his statement could be considered hasty and the punishment extreme – 'nevermore be officer of mine' – especially for a close friend (called Michael) as well as a recently appointed officer. Using a military punishment against Cassio partly because he disturbed Desdemona's rest demonstrates Othello's inability to keep the private and the public separate, though he promised the Senate he would be able to do so. The broken bond between Othello and Cassio (who is his link with Desdemona and respectable society) is the beginning of the end of Othello's reputation and of his marriage. From now on, Iago takes the place of Cassio. Iago once again shows expert knowledge of character, accurately predicting that Othello will overreact to the brawl and that Desdemona will exceed her brief and hold it a vice 'not to do more than she is requested'.

Act III scene 1

After a sleepless night Cassio brings musicians to play music for the awakening of the couple, but they are dismissed by Othello. Cassio tells Iago he has asked Emilia to arrange for him to see Desdemona. Emilia tells Cassio that she has overheard Othello say that Cassio will have to wait a while for the sake of decency, but he will be restored to his place at the first opportunity. However, Cassio still insists on speaking to Desdemona alone.

This brief and apparently redundant scene actually serves to reinforce Cassio's rejection by Othello, who ominously dismisses the musicians hired by Cassio as a celebration of the consummation. It is another example of how bedroom intimacy between Othello and Desdemona is disturbed by external noise, an invasion of the private by the public, love by war, as Othello goes off to inspect fortifications instead. Since an appreciation of gentle music was considered to be a noble and civilising attribute, it may be significant that Othello does not care for it, preferring the trumpeting of war. The Clown, in a Iago-like way, brings Desdemona down from her pedestal to the low level of lewd imaginings and indulges in instances of **double entendre** of a bestial nature with his talk of 'tails'. Cassio's lack of judgement and insistence on seeing Desdemona, even after he has been told that Othello does not intend to keep him permanently in disfavour, shows an inability to know when to practise patience, linking him to both Othello and Desdemona.

Act III scene 2

Othello does his job of attending to the fortification of the island.

This creates an ironic counterpoint to his personal invasion by the enemy in the following scene.

Act III scene 3

Desdemona assures Cassio, with Emilia as a witness, that she will pursue his cause. Iago points out to Othello Cassio's hasty departure on their arrival. Desdemona starts to pressurise Othello into seeing Cassio in order to reinstate him. He gives way to her but then tells her to leave him. Iago cleverly introduces to Othello the idea of his wife's infidelity with Cassio. As a result Othello asks that Emilia spy on

Desdemona. When Desdemona returns, he complains of a headache and she produces her handkerchief to bind it, but drops it unnoticed. Emilia picks it up and gives it to Iago, who had previously asked for it, and now conceives a use for it. Othello returns alone to continue the dialogue with Iago. He is tortured by visions of Desdemona with Cassio and makes a highly elaborate farewell to war and the old Othello. He demands proof from Iago to confirm his distrust. Iago tells him that Cassio revealed his intimacy with Desdemona in a dream heard by himself, and then mentions that Cassio has Desdemona's handkerchief, which was given to her by Othello. Othello summons the evil spirits of 'black vengeance' and allies himself to his new lieutenant, Iago, who swears loyalty to 'wronged Othello's service' and to kill Cassio if Othello will kill Desdemona.

This is one of the longest scenes in Shakespeare, having 480 lines and entrances and exits which would normally be marked by a scene change. Shakespeare has to keep up the relentless pace to remove opportunity for questions to creep into Othello's mind or for him to meet Cassio and Desdemona during this onslaught. This is known to critics as the temptation – or corruption – scene. The temptation, as with the apple in Eden, is of forbidden knowledge; Iago knows something which Othello doesn't, which drives him mad, first with curiosity and then with doubt. Othello cannot bear to 'know't a little' and becomes obsessed with the need to know more, which was Eve's original sin. Iago is lucky to find himself alone with Othello at this key moment, which may be attributed to Desdemona having gone too far in her insistent demands on Cassio's behalf and his needing a bit of peace. Again, this suggests the division between them. Desdemona aids Iago's case by being excessive, and therefore arousing suspicion. She also criticises Othello for 'mammering on', and makes an unfortunate connection between Cassio and wooing by using the ambiguous word 'suitor'. Othello also paves the way for Iago's assault by saying that without Desdemona's love 'Chaos is come again'. This is the first time Othello has admitted to a vulnerability or dependency, and this rising fear prepares him mentally for Iago to prey upon his dread of loss of that which has given his life light and direction. In his soliloquy, Othello starts to see himself as Iago sees him – black, unmannered and old (the opposite of Cassio) – and to succumb to the view (lines 384–85) that white tends to blackness.

Iago dominates the dialogue by controlling its content, by having more lines, and by imposing his animal diction. He has won the battle between the orators: Othello's speeches have not only become short but repetitive, grammatically incomplete and highly exclamatory – even inarticulate. The word 'satisfaction' is used several times in this scene by Iago, who gives it a sexual connotation as well as the meaning of satisfying curiosity with knowledge; he taunts Othello with it in both senses. Othello and Iago share lines as well as diction throughout this scene, indicating the bond forming between them. Much use is made by Iago of words relating to vision, working on Othello's imagination and a need for 'ocular proof'. Othello sets up his own imprisoning process of thinking and acting when he avows 'I'll see before I doubt; when I doubt, prove/And on the proof…Away at once with love or jealousy!' This may seem reasonable, but it excludes the essential stage in the pursuit of truth of speaking to the accused to check if there is another point of view or explanation. There is also the logistical problem of proving a positive: one can prove adultery, but not fidelity, and there is no one to present the case for the defence. Othello seems more bothered by shared possession of Desdemona, which damages his public honour, than by the hurt of private betrayal (lines 265–70). Once evil spirits are conjured, the process can no more be reversed than the 'compulsive course' of the sea with which Othello again identifies himself (lines 450–57).

At this central point in the play Othello starts to become Iago, sharing his barnyard view of sex and his misogyny. The visual effect of Othello and Iago kneeling is strikingly symbolic of how Othello has been brought low by Iago. Their ritual oath is a sealing of a contract with the devil: 'I am your own for ever' says Iago, taking possession of Othello in a travesty of a wedding ceremony. Desdemona has been replaced as Othello's soul mate and partner by Iago the magus, master, teacher and adviser. Othello becomes his dependent slave, playing the female role to Iago in the same way Cassio and Roderigo are forced to because of his apparent superior knowledge. As the *Arden* introduction puts it, 'Othello is almost the ventriloquist's dummy' and 'Faustus belongs to his servant-master Mephistopheles'. Iago could not have asked for the handkerchief 'a hundred times' and previously had no need of it – unless he wanted it in case an opportunity to make malicious use of it presented itself. Iago knows what is precious to others and how he can gain power over them through what they value.

There is a big question about how much Emilia realises about her husband's true character and his intentions for the handkerchief. That she tries to please him, even at the expense of upsetting her mistress, and though he treats her contemptuously, reflects the subordinate position of women at the time. Claiming that Cassio's cashiering grieves her husband (line 3) suggests that she is in fact fooled by him and that he misleads her about his real attitudes to others. When Iago dismisses his wife in line 317, it echoes Othello's dismissal of Desdemona at the beginning of the scene and brings the two marriages into parallel. In this scene Othello's mind turns from blissful trust to almost confirmed suspicion, without going through the safeguard, so important in *Hamlet*, of reflection. He is already too firmly in Iago's clutches ever to regain the former position, and one only asks for proof when a doubt has already been established. In this state of mind all future apparent evidence will be twisted to fit the hypothesis until it becomes a certainty. The headache is symbolic of Othello having accepted Iago's offer of the part of cuckold, visually represented by horns. One of many ironies in this scene, and one which hangs over the rest of the play, is that the loss of the handkerchief is caused not by Desdemona but by Othello himself, who pushes it away as a rejection of her love and concern.

Act III scene 4

Desdemona sends the Clown to fetch Cassio. She laments to Emilia the loss of the handkerchief. Othello arrives and asks to see it, telling her it is a magic handkerchief.

Desdemona lies about its whereabouts, and counters his demands for her to produce it with her own insistence that he reinstate Cassio. Othello walks out in a rage as Iago and Cassio enter. Cassio wants to know without further delay whether he will be readmitted to Othello's service. Desdemona admits that Othello is not himself, which she blames on state matters, though Emilia is unconvinced. Bianca complains to Cassio about his neglect of her, and he asks her to copy the handkerchief which he has found in his bedroom.

There is a breakdown in communication between Othello and Desdemona and a revelation of lack of understanding of each other's characters. Lying in both senses has become a dominant theme, and seems to be catching. Desdemona responds like a frightened child to Othello's demand, with non-committal and panicked answers and attempts to change the subject. The tale about the handkerchief may be another of Othello's romantic and dramatic fictions. His apparent belief in its magic, however, shows a pagan belief in the supernatural at odds with the other Othello of Act 1 with his respect for reason, and his hidden past is surfacing. We know he knows she hasn't got the handkerchief, and we see his bullying as bordering on sadistic torture, on a par with Iago's behaviour. The couple seem obsessive and excessive during their battle of demands between the handkerchief and Cassio, subjects now permanently linked in Othello's mind. We see the contrast between the worldly Emilia – who has had experience of marriage, men and their jealousy – and her naïve mistress. Cassio's insistence on knowing about his reinstatement reinforces the idea that not knowing is painful, and he is extreme in his demand and careless of the cost to Desdemona. He speaks formally and respectfully to Desdemona, who can aid him, but slightingly to Bianca, with whom he satisfies his appetites after dark. It is deceitful of him not to want Othello to see him 'womaned'. Like the other two men, he dismisses his woman and asks to be left alone. Telling Bianca 'Not that I love you not' has the devious circumlocution of a Iago utterance, and in this scene the audience starts to wonder whether Cassio is really so different from Iago beneath his gentlemanly manners and exterior. Emilia's lie 'I know not, madam' is a crucial thematic utterance in the play and the last point at which the tragedy could have been averted by truth.

Act IV scene 1

Iago continues where he left off in Act III scene 3, forcing Othello to discuss the handkerchief and Desdemona's honesty. He claims Cassio has admitted the affair to him, provoking Othello to fall into a fit. Cassio appears during it but Iago gets rid of him quickly. When Cassio returns it is to be an unwitting performer in a charade engineered by Iago, with Othello as spectator, whereby Bianca is substituted for Desdemona as the topic of conversation. Bianca appears in person at this point, and throws back the handkerchief in sight of Othello. Cassio chases after her, which gives Iago the opportunity to move Othello on to the point of settling that Desdemona and Cassio will die the same evening. Officials from Venice, relatives of Desdemona, arrive with a letter for Othello, in front of whom he strikes her. The shocked Lodovico is told by Iago that this is typical of Othello's current behaviour.

This is the best example of 'seeing is believing' in the play. Iago is firmly in control in this scene, and its play within a play created by himself. He initiates and directs the action and reactions, timings of entrances and exits and the pat delivery of lines with attendant body language. Othello has now been reduced to a common spy, and one who falsely interprets what he sees. He has fallen so low as to be writhing on the ground, with triumphant Iago looking down on him and sadistically enjoying his de-creation of the great general, who is now no better than Roderigo, a dog on a leash who obeys commands. In his ascendancy Iago no longer even pretends to address Othello respectfully, but tells him to be a man and pull himself together. Othello's speech, or rather raving rant (lines 35–43), is full of question and exclamation marks, obsessive repetition and lapses of syntax. This linguistic breakdown reflects his mental collapse, as does his falling to the ground in a fit of 'savage madness'. Noses and lips are surrogate genitals, and once again Othello is at the mercy of his visual imagination. The scene ends in prose, another sign of a falling off. By line 254 Othello's speech has become even more incoherent and disjointed, and schizophrenically polarised into the private and public modes, the old and the new Othello. His reference to 'Goats and monkeys!' (line 265) apes Iago's phrase of III.3.400, and indicates how far Iago has succeeded in implanting words and visions into Othello's mind.

Iago has the luck of the devil in that Bianca turns up to reject the handkerchief at the opportune moment, unwittingly confirming Desdemona's death sentence. He even knows that Cassio can be counted upon to laugh excessively. His addressing Cassio as Lieutenant is sadistic malice. Cassio calls Bianca a 'bauble' and the audience sees more of his double standards regarding women. Iago persuades Othello to 'strangle her in her bed' rather than use poison. There are many possible reasons for this: Iago needs to see a woman dead in 'the bed she hath contaminated' for his own psychological reasons; he considers it a more barbaric form of death; it will cause more suffering to both parties; it will make Othello's guilt the greater; strangulation is a military assault in which the stronger prevails; it is a travesty of the act of love to kill in bed with a pillow. The arrival of the Venetians to relieve Othello and to promote Cassio – although logical since the Turkish threat has been temporarily removed – seems to be an indictment of Othello and a confirmation of Cassio as his replacement in love and war. Striking a woman was regarded as cowardly and dishonourable at the time, especially in public, and this action damages both their reputations. Like Iago, Othello now assumes all men want to sleep with his wife, and accuses Lodovico of this – even though he is her kinsman – with much emphasis on the thematic word 'turn'.

Act IV scene 2

Othello interrogates Emilia about Desdemona's alleged meetings with Cassio. She denies them but Othello doesn't believe her. Desdemona swears her innocence to

Othello, again to no avail. He insults Emilia and Desdemona by giving them money as he leaves. She asks Emilia to put her wedding sheets on the bed and weeps in front of Iago about losing her lord. Roderigo demands the return of his jewellery, which Iago pretended to have given to Desdemona, and states his intention to stop his 'unlawful solicitation' of her. Iago promises he will enjoy Desdemona the following night (when he knows she will be dead) if he kills Cassio.

Known as the brothel scene, this episode is an example of how evidence can only confirm a suspicion, not dislodge it; Emilia's truth seems the same as if she were telling lies. Desdemona kneels to Othello, an image of pathos, childlike vulnerability, subservience, and a reminder of the unholy alliance between himself and Iago. Othello seems to have fallen into self-pity for being a figure of scorn. He uses base imagery of smell, hell, weeds and reptiles/insects. Iago again tries to stop his wife's mouth, a preview of the final scene. His being kneeled to by Desdemona is a grotesque irony and echo (line 150). There is feasting and entertaining of the Venetians as an ironic public background to the private horror. 'Is't possible?' (line 86) is the question which haunts the play, and to which Iago provides answers on many levels. Iago, whose prior knowledge is usually accurate, says Othello is being sent to Mauretania in Africa; there would have been no military reason for the Senate to post him there – it having no connection with the Venetian empire – but there is a symbolism in his not being recalled to Venice but returned to the imagined original homeland of Moors at that time, and in Desdemona's not being allowed to return home; perhaps Brabantio's influence is at work, as she herself suggests. The wedding sheets are about to become winding sheets, as her marital bed becomes her grave (as in *Romeo and Juliet*). Critics disagree over the tone of lines 106–08, which may be either sarcastic (but out of character) or docilely accepting blame; since she refers to the meaning of her name – 'wretched fortune' (line 127) – it is possible she is simply being fatalistic.

Act IV scene 3

It is night and Othello orders Desdemona to go to bed, dismiss Emilia and wait for him. As she is being prepared for bed, Desdemona sings a death song. Emilia disagrees with Desdemona that adultery could never be justified, but blames men for women's faults.

In what is known as the Willow Scene, a scene of high tension and pathos, the wives are forced into a bond of ignorance and passivity, as a contrasting parallel to that between their husbands. There is a flow of warmth and tenderness between Desdemona and Emilia which is ironic in many different ways. Emilia has taken on the dominant role of mother (as Iago has 'fathered' Othello), soothing, counselling and undressing, while Desdemona in her white nightdress is the pious and vulnerable child at bedtime, as well as the virgin sacrifice being prepared. Desdemona thinks she is preparing for love but is in fact preparing for death, which is emphasised by the gothic atmosphere – complete with superstition, a wind, and phantom knocking at the door. Barbary's tragic song, with prophetic references to the death of a woman caused by the betrayal of her lover, is Desdemona's **swan song**. Perhaps her mother's maid was black, but in any case her name seems too coincidental not to be an oblique reference to the Berbers or Moors and victimisation. By taking on the persona of a maid perhaps Desdemona is suggesting that all women are handmaids to men, whatever their social status. In a scene reminiscent of a gothic horror story, she has become a fictional romantic character after all. Emilia's relative morality, which ironically highlights Desdemona's purity and innocence, hints at a self-interest stemming from her husband's influence.

Act V scene 1

In the darkness, Iago conducts Roderigo's attack on Cassio, who is returning from Bianca's house. It is Iago's intention that both men should die to prevent the truth from being revealed. Roderigo fails and is instead wounded by Cassio, who receives a leg injury from Iago before the latter exits. Othello can hear the fight and assumes Cassio has been killed as planned. After Lodovico and Gratiano have heard the cries of the two wounded, Iago re-enters bearing a light and offers help to Cassio, whilst also taking the opportunity to stab Roderigo. When Bianca appears, Iago points to her fright and paleness as evidence of her conspiracy in the attack on Cassio. Emilia turns up, insults Bianca and is instructed by Iago to inform Othello and Desdemona what has happened, though he presumably does not expect Desdemona still to be alive.

Everyone is a villain, victim, witness or suspect in Iago's 'play'. It has been suggested that Iago starts making mistakes here, or that his run of luck has finished, though he would still be in the clear as long as Roderigo died, and once Othello has become a murderer his accusations will not carry much weight. Again Othello misinterprets the action, mistaking the voice of Roderigo for Cassio. His retiring couplet (lines 35–36) is that of a stereotypical stage villain, and exaggerated in that he is going to strangle her, not spill her blood. Roderigo's naming of Iago as 'inhuman dog' (a Turk) is the first time Iago has been seen for what he is. His envy of Cassio's 'daily beauty' suggests that Cassio has been an equally prime target all along, and that Iago knows what 'beauty' is and resents being deprived of it, though he has up to now denied the existence of such an abstract and effeminate concept, along with love, honour and reputation. It is obviously ironic that Iago should be a light-bearer, and that once again he should offer support to Cassio and concern for his 'dear friend' Roderigo. He quickly turns appearance (Bianca's) into evidence for a situation which is plausible but false. Bianca pointedly claims to be as honest as Emilia. Iago's final couplet is evidence of his addiction to gambling.

Act V scene 2

Othello enters the bedroom and kisses the sleeping Desdemona while justifying what he intends to do. She wakes and he warns her that he is about to kill her so she had better say her prayers. She asks that Cassio be sent for to testify on her behalf, but is told that he is dead. She begs for more time but Othello refuses and smothers her. Emilia arrives too late to prevent Desdemona's death but in time to hear Desdemona claim it was not Othello's fault. Emilia is thunderstruck to be told by Othello that 'honest, honest Iago' was the person who claimed Desdemona was false. She rails at Othello for his ignorance and stupidity, and also verbally attacks her husband when he confirms his slander, despite his ordering her to be quiet. Gratiano delivers the news that Brabantio is dead. When Emilia explains how Cassio got the handkerchief, Othello tries to kill Iago but is disarmed, and Iago gets the opportunity to stab Emilia and run away. Montano chases Iago while Gratiano keeps guard outside the bedroom door. Emilia dies singing the Willow Song and vouching for Desdemona's love for the 'cruel Moor'. Othello finds another sword and calls Gratiano in to witness his speech of self-damnation, an audience then swelled by Lodovico, Cassio, Montano and Iago. Iago refuses to satisfy Othello's need to know the cause of his hatred. Written evidence is produced against Iago from dead Roderigo's pockets. Cassio is to be governor in Cyprus, Iago is to be tortured by him, and Othello is to be taken back to Venice for trial, but he prevents this by killing himself in military fashion. He falls upon the bed with the bodies of Desdemona and Emilia.

Dr Johnson found this scene to be so moving as to be unendurable, and another critic called it 'unutterable agony'; it has been said that it pushes the limits of what can be shown on stage. All that was white has been besmirched with blackness, and 'chaos is come again', with much light/dark imagery to emphasise this. With the announcement that 'yonder foul murder's done' the public and private, war and love, Christian and Turk are subsumed into each other. Othello, who took on the role of Desdemona's protector, and for whom she is waiting like a little girl wanting to be tucked up and kissed goodnight, is doubly betrayed by her husband and father figure, who asks if she has said her prayers – a travesty of parental concern. We have not seen him for a while and he has a semblance of calm, which proves to be false: Desdemona comments on his gnawing his lip, his rolling eyes and his 'bloody passion', and he is overcome with wrath when she weeps for Cassio's supposed murder. Emilia is forthright in her condemnation of Othello's act and her racism emerges in the language of 'dirt'. It is her tragedy as well as Othello's and Desdemona's; she made a mistake, sees a loved one dead, and ends by bravely defying slander and conspiracy at the cost of her life.

Othello's claim to be protecting other men by killing Desdemona (cf the Willow Song's 'You'll couch with moe men') is either self-delusion or an indication that he, like Iago, now sees this as a gender war. His forcing her down on the bed, lying on top of her and silencing her in a breathless spasm is a horrible travesty of the consummation the previous night. (The verb 'die' was used then as a term for orgasm.) It is an un-Christian act which jeopardises both their souls: he kills her in a moment of wrath, provoked by another visual misinterpretation (her tears), and does not allow her time to pray.

Iago, who feels confident that he cannot be blamed for someone else's foolish credulity, makes the mistake of thinking he can rely on his wife's continuing obedience to stay silent; it is fitting that he should be undone by a woman, and by his dupe Roderigo, who has convenient (albeit unlikely) letters in his pocket to convict Iago. Othello makes the appeal 'Iago knows' in line 209; but Iago withdraws his knowledge with 'what you know, you know' (line 300) – which is nothing. Iago's refusal to speak at the end is unusual in Shakespeare and seems unnatural for a man of words. He may be pushing Othello to suicide, which would guarantee Othello's damnation, would carry his plan to conclusion, and the death of the key witness would be to his own advantage. Iago's self-esteem would be damaged by any admission of envy or jealousy. Cassio's promotion at the end of the play, and himself alive to see it and suffer from it, is probably the worst possible punishment for Iago (or is it his exclusion from the trinity of loved ones on the bed?). Fortune's wheel turns quickly: the new governor of Cyprus is the recently dismissed lieutenant. Cassio's forgiveness and charity mark him out as the true Christian. That he is male, white and a gentleman restores the social order. Lodovico calls Othello 'rash' and 'unfortunate' – the victim of a combination of impetuosity and ill fate. Othello also blames fate ('ill-starred wench' and 'error of the moon') rather than himself; his claims to have loved 'too well' and to be an 'honourable murderer' are self-exculpating (the latter phrase is, according to the *Penguin* notes, said with 'bitter irony', but this is debatable). Surrendering to illusions and rewriting history has been his weakness, from first to last, and he may be doing it again now. He reverts to a legendary role of the valiant Christian killing the Turk, the enemy of his adopted state who is also his inner self. The act of murdering Desdemona meant killing the better (Christian) half of himself. This meant that he still has to deal with the enemy Turk, which he fails to do in his strangely unsuccessful attempts to kill the 'devil' Iago, but he succeeds by killing himself.

Traditionally, death is preferable to ignominious imprisonment for those with a sense of honour, so Othello has no option but to commit suicide. Othello ends as he has always lived, essentially alone, outnumbered and threatened with defeat. He requires an audience for his final tale, his grandiloquent egocentric farewell speech, full of the language of sea and battles, rhetoric and metaphor; the old Othello is back, in the third person, and insisting on the restoration of his reputation and his past. 'Well, thou dost best' (line 303) is an enigmatic utterance from Othello a few lines later. It is unlikely that this refers to Iago's decision never to speak again, as he does not address him in the second person after line 286, and it would not make a lot of sense in the context, but it seems unrelated to what Gratiano has just said and more relevant to his own decision. Othello's self-slaughter is paradoxically anti-Christian yet an attempt to prove he is one and, like Judas (the Folio text reads 'Iudean' not 'Indian' in line 343), he throws away the precious white pearl of his soul. There is another Christian reference in the 'med'cinable gum' in line 347, which is myrrh. Alternatively, his suicide can be seen as justice being executed on the guilty and an act of fit retribution. The play ends with this overwhelming vision of horror, which has to be screened from our eyes.

Characters

Dramatis personae

Othello is a Moor originating from Morocco via Spain. He has been a mercenary soldier since the age of 7, is probably now aged 42, and after various campaigns is a renowned general in the employ of the Venetian state. For 9 months he has been waiting in Venice for his next mission, and has passed the time by visiting Senator Brabantio's house to entertain him and, subsequently, his daughter (Desdemona), whom Othello has just secretly married. Iago is a long-time fellow soldier, but Othello has just appointed Michael Cassio as his lieutenant. Othello murders his wife because he becomes convinced that she has been having an affair with Cassio. He then commits suicide.

Desdemona, aged between 16 and 18 years old, is friendless and motherless. She has led a sheltered life of domestic duty under the watchful eye of her father, Brabantio. She is bowled over by the tales Othello tells of his military exploits and journeys, and conceives a desire to travel and experience the wider world. Her ill-fated name means 'the unfortunate' in Greek. She is murdered by her husband in bed.

Iago, presumably Venetian, is married, childless, and a veteran soldier. He is an 'ancient', meaning an ensign, a junior infantry officer whose traditional duty is to be the standard bearer, i.e. to carry the flag into battle. Iago is a Spanish name — like Othello and Roderigo — and that of the most famous saint in Spain, Sant'Iago, who was known as 'the Moor killer' for his slaughter of Spanish Moors. He is 28. He has previously suspected his wife (Emilia) of having a sexual liaison with both Othello and Cassio. He has been disappointed in his expectation of promotion, and now resents Cassio, whom he does not consider to merit the rank of lieutenant. He has a low opinion of women, and professes to hate the Moor. He exploits Roderigo, who pays him to advance his cause with Desdemona, and persuades him that Cassio is his rival. He incites Othello to turn against his new wife and best friend and to agree to their murders. He injures Cassio and kills both his own wife and Roderigo.

Cassio is a Florentine, making him, like Othello, a mercenary and an outsider. Florentines were considered to be of higher social standing because of the city's cultural reputation. He is a theoretical and inexperienced soldier, but chivalrous and educated: a gentleman by contrast to Othello and Iago. He is also good-looking and generally privileged. He has been a chaperone and go-between in the courtship of Desdemona by Othello. He has no head for drink, which makes him aggressive. He consorts with a Venetian courtesan, Bianca, in Cyprus. He is concerned about rank and honour, and is consistently an admirer of Othello, his superior officer, and of Desdemona. He becomes governor of Cyprus at the end and is made responsible for the torture of Iago.

Emilia is a Venetian designated to be maid to Desdemona and to travel to Cyprus in the company of her husband, Iago. She desires to please Iago, despite his questionable treatment of her in private and public. She becomes loyally attached to Desdemona despite having stolen her handkerchief and having lied about it.

Roderigo is a wealthy fool soon parted from his money, despised by Iago as 'poor trash of Venice' and rejected by Brabantio as a suitor for his daughter. He thinks he is in love with Desdemona and resents the fact that she has chosen a black man over himself. At Iago's instigation he sells his land and follows her to Cyprus. Iago uses him to discredit and attack Cassio, and then kills him when injured. Only on his death does he understand that Iago has exploited him, and that Desdemona never received his jewels or messages. He provides evidence against Iago before he dies.

Brabantio is a leading senator of a group of ten councillors, under the leadership of the Duke of Venice, responsible for governing the Venetian empire. He enjoys control and has a high opinion of his own status and the city-state of Venice. He has strong views on who is acceptable as a marriage partner for his only child, Desdemona, and he would rather disown his daughter than accept her marriage to a Moor. He dies of grief, for either his lost daughter or his lost reputation.

Bianca is part of the established Venetian community in Cyprus with her own lodgings. Cassio visits her there and she falls in love with him. She unwittingly plays a role in the damning of Desdemona with the missing handkerchief, as Cassio gives it to her to copy.

Othello, the Moor

Although he appears on stage much less than Iago, and to some audiences he is much less interesting than the villain, Othello is intended to be the main character of the eponymous play because Iago does not undergo change during the drama but Othello does, and to a great extent. Although it is caused by Iago, the focus of the dramatic interest is Othello's unravelling mind, and whether he and Desdemona can survive Iago's hate campaign. We can relate to Othello, although he is more distant and mysterious in many ways, better than we can relate to Iago, who eludes our understanding.

Two Othellos

There is an ambiguity about Othello, personified by the two Othellos we see in the play: although he is a servant to white masters and has primitive origins, he has a high rank, an aristrocratic bearing, and the civilised skills of rhetoric. It has been claimed that Othello and Iago are the two faces of man, the good and the evil in human nature, and, conversely, that they are the same man, both suffering from the same psychological and psychopathic disturbance triggered by the monster jealousy.

Another possibility — given that Shakespeare writes about real people, and real people do not always behave predictably and logically — is that Othello is meant to be a mass of inconsistencies, and he falls back on his buried childhood self when threatened and under pressure, as people tend to do.

There isn't even agreement on Othello's physical condition, as he can be seen as either a larger-than-life, peak-of-fitness, epitome of the conquering warrior, or a has-been suffering from his age and rusty after 9 months of soft living. Honigmann believes that he has impaired vision, and another critic has argued for his sexual impotence and the non-consummation of his marriage. At 42 he would be considered of advanced years (Shakespeare lived to be only 52), but the Senate obviously has every confidence in his physique and deems him 'all-in-all sufficient' (IV.1.267).

Othello's opinion of Iago could also be deemed ambivalent. If he thinks so highly of him, why does he not make Iago his lieutenant? Iago has served Othello for many years and seems to have expected the promotion, though in that case his employment of mediators is odd. Perhaps Othello does not consider Iago to be officer material, since he does not have the manners of a gentleman. He may have been annoyed by the pressure which was put upon him by the three influential Venetians to choose Iago. Cassio comes from the background and class which Othello is aspiring to by his liaison with Desdemona, and would reflect well on his superior officer, for whom he deputises. Othello may feel that Cassio deserves the job for his role of chaperone and go-between during the 9-month secret courtship, as a reward for his discretion, loyalty and silence. We know that Othello believes unquestioningly in Iago's honesty, but we do not know how he feels about his ambitions.

Noble Othello?

The question which divided critics throughout the twentieth century was whether Othello is a noble hero deceived by a superhumanly cunning Iago, or a deeply-flawed egotist responsible for his own downfall. Iago mocks him for being weak and a 'credulous fool'; and when he says 'He's that he is' (IV.I.272) — meaning violent, irrational and unable to control his passions — he is suggesting that this is the Moor's essential, savage nature. Elsewhere, however, Iago lists his virtues.

A. C. Bradley presented the case in 1904 for Othello being a noble hero worthy of our sympathy who, without Iago's interference, would have led a blameless existence. F. R. Leavis in 1952 argued against this view, asserting that Othello is neither noble nor a hero, that Iago could not have had an effect if the character weaknesses were not already there, and that therefore Othello cannot be admirable. Because Bradley claims that the proof of Othello's nobility lies in his capacity for absolute trust, the debate focuses on whether Othello really trusts Desdemona, as he claims to when he has her sent for and swears 'My life upon her faith!' (I.3.291).

For it to evaporate so quickly suggests he never really trusted her; or that like religious faith and love, which are also irrational, trust, when put to the test, can go as suddenly as it comes; or that jealousy is stronger than trust and will always defeat it. A trust which can be destroyed in less than 20 minutes is obviously flawed in some way, however, and by contrast Desdemona never loses hers. The debate continues.

It is essential to Othello's self-esteem to believe himself noble and have others believe it too, as honour is inseparable from nobility. He fulfils the criteria by being successful, respected by his subordinates and superiors and entrusted with the safety of the republic of Venice. He is poetic, sensitive to nature, dedicated to his job and his religion. His entry into the play is impressive and carries authority, as does his speech to the Senate, which wins an accolade from the Duke. He is familiar with the concepts of duty and salvation, justice and love, and with their importance. His reputation is for having a 'solid virtue' and a 'nature/Whom passion could not shake' (IV.1.267–68). Even Iago refers to his 'noble nature' (II.1.280).

However, there is also evidence for the claim that Othello is lacking in nobility. He displays an emotional volatility and exceptional sensuousness which would not be consistent with the contemporary view of how a noble character would behave, and consideration for others is not a character trait even his greatest admirers could claim for him. Lodovico calls him 'rash', as well as admitting that he is 'most unfortunate'. There are elements of excess in his make-up, and he could be accused of excessive love for Desdemona. Brabantio charges him with being a 'foul thief', and it is questionable how noble it is to marry secretly without permission. Striking a woman, and in public, was an indisputably ignoble act at the time; killing Desdemona is a violation against chivalry as well as of Christian principles. He could be seen as fitting the swaggering soldier stereotype known as 'Braggadocio' in Elizabethan literature; as Iago puts it, he won Desdemona 'for bragging and telling her fantastical lies' (II.1.217). When Othello says 'Cuckold me!', 'False to me!', 'And with mine officer!' there is a strong indication of pride and arrogance. Most damning is that he falls early on into one of the deadliest of the **seven deadly sins**, wrath. Paradoxically, the strongest evidence against his nobility is also the strongest evidence for it: Leavis says he is is stupid because he is credulous, but, as Chapman says, 'noblest natures are most credulous'. This is a vicious circle, well-documented in Shakespeare's plays, whereby a surfeit of a virtue becomes harmful.

Tempting fate

The Elizabethans were familiar with the figure of 'the over-reacher', a dramatic character who aims too high and therefore falls below human level. Othello could be accused of **hubris**, of wanting to be god-like, in his insistence on knowing more than he should want to know or is capable of bearing. He is over-confident in his belief in his abilities and judgement, and that his passions and appetites are under control. He has the arrogance to believe he can take on and out-talk Brabantio, the second most important man in Venice, and offend Venetian sensibilities with impunity. He is tempting fate when he swears 'My life upon her faith' about a woman he doesn't really know very well, and to her father. In short, he could be said to be heading for the fall of the tragic hero, which in his case takes the ironic form of his turning Turk, the lowest and most despised creature he can imagine, and against whom he has spent his whole life fighting.

True love?

There is doubt about the validity of Othello and Desdemona's relationship in that it arose from Desdemona's forwardness in offering herself as available for courtship, and was based on the sharing of glamorous fictionalised war stories and the linked roles of storyteller and listener. He loves her for pitying his dangers, which may not be a solid base for a marriage. Leavis thinks: 'It may be love, but it can be only in an oddly qualified sense love of her: it must be much more a matter of self-centred and self-regarding satisfactions — pride, sensual possessiveness, appetite, love of loving — than he suspects.' He seems dependent on her to keep chaos at bay, but again that is not the same as love. The only evidence for his loving her is that he says he does, and says so in the traditional poetic language of lovers, and that Desdemona believes he does. But the audience cannot be certain, since the characters themselves cannot be trusted to know.

Othello's languages

Roderigo describes Othello very early on as a 'wheeling and extravagant stranger' (I.1.137), presumably meaning that he was perceived by Venetians as exotic and extreme in his language as well as his in appearance. Heilman portrays Othello as being addicted to 'rhetorical bravura' and Clemen describes him as the speaker of 'bright, colourful, intense pictures'. His speeches to the Senate in Act I scene 3 are grandiose public speaking, full of metaphor, hyperbole and the traditional archaisms and euphemisms of military diction, such as 'steed'. His imagery is sensuous, cosmic and elemental, relating to movement and size; it carries him away, and his listeners. He commonly uses the first person pronoun and is egocentric in his relating of events and feelings.

Later in the play his utterances become very different. Here is a selection: 'Ha!'; 'O misery!'; 'Not a jot, not a jot'; 'Ha, ha, false to me!'; 'Death and damnation! O!'; 'O monstrous! Monstrous!'; 'I'll tear her all to pieces!'; 'O, blood, blood, blood!'; 'The handkerchief!'; 'Zounds!'; 'What? What?'; 'O, I see that nose of yours, but not that dog I shall throw it to!'; 'but yet the pity of it, Iago! O, Iago, the pity of it, Iago!'; 'I will chop her into messes!'; 'Fire and brimstone!'; 'I am glad to see you mad.'

In the second half of Act III (from III.3.154) until he leaves in Act IV scene 2, Othello's speech reflects his wrath, mental pain and dependency on Iago, whose diction he is copying. Humans are reduced to 'Goats and monkeys!' The epileptic fit speech (IV.1.35–43) and the one after he strikes Desdemona (IV.1.254–65) contain examples of most of the features of his growing inarticulacy: very short responses; simple or non-sentences; non-words; repetition; monosyllables; grammatical breakdown; contradiction; exclamation; cursing. His blasphemous language echoes Iago's first word in the play: ''Sblood.' Now he sees himself from the outside, through Iago's eyes, imagining that Desdemona shares this view, and his shaken confidence is indicated in his fractured utterance and the loss of his former fluency and rhetoric. The content is a mixture of religious rant, violent threat and the grossly sexual, fixed on things of the flesh.

Racial stereotype

All the characters call Othello 'the Moor', even Desdemona sometimes, drawing attention to his race. Comments are made or implied about his sexual appetite and performance (which he feels obliged to deny to the Duke); when Iago makes these comments, he frames them in gross animal terms. (Shakespeare's other Moors are associated with sexual desire for white virgins.) Another accusation made against blacks was that they were incapable of reason, because they were primitive and undisciplined, and that they indulged in sensuality and unbridled emotion. Othello has a tendency to weep and roar, with exaggerated physical mannerisms, and there is an emphasis in the play on Othello's sense of smell and taste which links him to bestial instincts and appetites. Iago's intention to lead him 'by the nose as asses are' reminds us of slavery and beasts of burden.

Othello makes many references to elemental forces of nature, such as the sea and moon, which suggests a paganism beneath his Christianity. The stereotype also included the idea that non-whites were childishly unstable in mood and feelings: 'these Moors are changeable in their wills' (Iago I.3.342–43). Othello's language and behaviour reveal a bloodthirsty disposition and savouring of violence, and he could be said to revert to primitive beliefs and instincts and lose the veneer of civilisation when under pressure, as shown by the handkerchief story and reaction to its loss. He does not seem comfortable in society or indoors. He also conforms to the racial stereotype of the fierce warrior of royal descent, capable of charming and overawing men and women with his grand presence and exotic appearance, but broodingly dangerous.

Racial hostility

Othello's appearance in the play is delayed until three hostile characters — Iago, Roderigo and Brabantio, a cross-section of Venetian society — have given their condemnatory views of him, which make Othello a victim from the start. There are specific verbal racist insults used in the play: 'thick-lips' (Roderigo I.1.67); 'old black ram' (I.1.89); 'the devil' (I.1.92); 'a Barbary horse' (I.1.112); 'sooty bosom'

(Brabantio I.2.70); 'most filthy bargain' (Emilia V.2.156). Iago, as ever, is more subtle and his abuse takes the form of gratuitous mention of his colour ('black Othello' II.3.29), constant reference to him as 'the Moor', and lascivious comments on his sexuality. Othello's consciousness of his race may be a factor in his character and behaviour; perhaps only pretending to be confident, he may suffer from being 'the outsider'. Knowing that people talk about him behind his back and disapprove of him, might make him insecure and quick to think the worst. It certainly makes him dependent on the insider knowledge of a Venetian about other Venetians. Othello's willingness to listen to Iago later, and even make him into his adviser and look up to him, may stem more from Othello's fear and isolation — having lost Cassio — than from his respect for Iago's perception and intelligence. Iago's apparently honest face is, ironically, the only thing which Othello feels able to trust in a hostile world, and which belongs to his past before Venice and the sudden change in his life. His secret marriage suggests he knows perfectly well that Brabantio does not, in fact, love him and would not have given consent. It could be said that he seems to have a need to make himself subservient, whether to the Duke, Desdemona or Iago. Though they speak of his military reputation, his worth to the state and his narrative skill, no one says anything to suggest that they value him as a man. Since Brabantio describes Othello in public as a practitioner of black magic and implies he is a 'pagan' and a 'bondslave' (I.2.99), this must have some effect on Othello's self-esteem.

Racism rather than race could be said to be the cause of Othello's downfall in that his insecurities — the basis of his jealousy, and fears of cuckoldry and of loss of honour — may have been fostered by the racist treatment he has received. Only Desdemona and Cassio have been personally chosen by him as trusted supporters, so it is obviously devastating when both of them seem to have turned against him. Even Desdemona, by stating that she sees his 'visage in his mind', tacitly admits that he does not have a socially acceptable outward visage.

Either Iago, if he is lying, or the Senate, if he is telling the truth, thinks Othello should be sent to Mauritania, in Africa, rather than recalled to Venice (IV.2.223); sending them back to where they came from is the time-honoured way of dealing with unwanted immigrants. Othello may well have been upset by the letters from Venice if they added professional to personal failure. When the Cyprus crisis did not materialise and their need of Othello was diminished, Brabantio may have been able to persuade the rest of the Senate to punish him for his presumption in secretly marrying a white woman of high society. Desdemona thinks this is what has happened (IV.2.46). As in the case of Richard III, regarded as evil because of his hunchback, the prejudices of society and their application make it difficult or pointless not to conform to everyone's worst assumptions and expectations.

The other view

Shakespeare discourages a one-sided interpretation of *Othello* as a warning against mixed marriage or a condemnation of Moors. By making his main character an experienced commander and accomplished warrior who is physically impressive, attractive to men and women, poetic, imaginative, a devout Christian, powerful orator and implacable enemy of 'the Ottomites', Shakespeare opposes or offsets cultural misconceptions. Since Iago is the metaphorical Turk, monster and 'black' man, Shakespeare is reversing the racist prejudice of his time that evil is indicated by skin colour. By calling a courtesan Bianca, he is drawing attention to the complexities and ironies of distinguishing black from white. The Duke tells Brabantio his 'son-in-law is far more fair than black' (I.3.287). There are other characters with the same faults as Othello, such as wrath, jealousy and credulity. There is a lack of Christian attitude and behaviour in Brabantio, Roderigo, Emilia and, obviously, Iago which casts ironic doubt upon the alleged superiority of their culture, and one can only see Othello through their eyes if one is prepared to adopt a racist viewpoint.

Final moments

Othello's last speech is argued over by critics, who see it as either a return to the former glory of the Othello of Act I scene 3, or a return to his original error of solipsism and putting a 'romantic glamour' (Wilson Knight) on bloody reality. T. S. Eliot controversially claimed that it is a speech of self-exculpation and making excuses, and that Othello has not achieved 'greater self-knowledge' but is trying to cheer himself up.

His death gets him out of an embarrassing and awkward situation, caught with the body and the only alternative to self-inflicted death being taken back as a prisoner to public dishonour in Venice. The question is whether to interpret the suicide as honourable and just self-punishment — ignoring the anti-Christian nature of the act — which re-establishes him in the good opinion of the audience off and on stage (who expected him to try to do it because 'he was great of heart' (V.2.357)), or whether to see it as a self-deluding assertion that he is better than the Turk and a way of showing off to remind the Venetians that he has 'done the state some service' and isn't just a common murderer. The paradox remains that the Christian Othello claims to be destroying the pagan one, yet his suicide is a sinful act of violence which traduces the state and makes him indistinguishable from 'the circumcisèd dog'.

Honest Iago

Generations of students have found Iago a fascinating character who steals the show and is the main focus of watching and studying the play. He gets 1,097 lines to Othello's 887, is on stage almost continuously and much more than anyone else, and he knows and interacts with all the other characters, high and low.

Evil charm

If evil were not attractive, it would not be dangerous. Evil in literature is always more interesting than goodness, since evil generates individuality, excitement, passion, fear and everything else which creates drama. Iago is Satanic in his energy, intelligence and daring contempt for goodness. He also has, uniquely in the play, a sense of humour, a device which always wins audiences. We cannot help admiring his daring and quick-thinking, while knowing we should disapprove of his amorality. The gambler is always a fascinating character, as there is the suspense of how far he is prepared to go and when his luck will change. 'Lucky' is perhaps a more appropriate fixed epithet than 'honest', since Iago has the luck of the devil and chance always seems to be on his side. Timing favours Iago throughout, as do outcomes: 'consequence do but approve my dream' (II.3.58). Many events could not have been caused by Iago, but just fell out as he would have wished, e.g. Cassio and Montano declining to speak after the fight, Cassio sneaking away 'guilty-like' and Emilia finding the dropped handkerchief. Other actions by the characters are more a matter of his being able to predict their responses through clever guesswork based on a knowledge of how their minds work, but which nonetheless makes them fall neatly into his trap, such as Brabantio's rejection of his daughter, Cassio's liking for pretty things, and Desdemona's overdoing the pleading for Cassio's reinstatement.

Cynical youth

Iago states that he is 28 years old (I.3.308–09), which students usually find surprising. It is shocking for one so young to be so hard and cynical, as it seems he cannot have had enough disillusionments to justify such a low view of humanity, or be experienced enough to think he understands all the ways of the world. It is also worrying that he can treat his young wife with such contempt, as though he got tired of her many years ago, or view his senior in age, Othello, as his inferior in a culture which respected age and the wisdom thought to accompany it. Iago's comparative youth (though not as relatively young as 28 would be nowadays) seems unnatural for someone of his views and makes him the more alarming to the audience, while disarming the characters and helping to explain why they do not see through him. Directors often present him as being much older.

Primary target

Iago appears to have reasons for hating all of the other main characters, so there is a question concerning his main target. Leaving aside the homosexual argument, since Shakespeare prefers things much less clear-cut than this approach would imply (which is not to say there are not some elements of homosexuality in Iago's complex make-up which affect his feelings towards both Cassio and Othello), the hatred seems equally intense towards Othello, Cassio and Desdemona, all of whom he both despises and envies for different reasons. According to Bradley, Iago has a 'keen sense of superiority' which is thwarted and wants satisfaction, and his guiding resentment is of 'Othello's eminence, Othello's goodness, and his own dependence on Othello', so he makes his superiors his puppets. The racial hatred for Othello is paralleled by a political hatred for the 'Florentine' Cassio, and there is equally strong misogyny to account for his need to defeat Desdemona. In some ways Cassio, with a 'daily beauty in his life', most threatens Iago's position and self-esteem, as he can be most directly compared to him and found wanting as a fellow soldier, peer and white man. By the end of the play his target has become anyone who stands in the way of the execution of his plan to destroy lives and get away with it.

Losing the plot
Critics question whether Iago loses sight of his original intentions at some stage in the play. His first plan is only to cause Othello trouble by rousing Brabantio, and it seems as if it is his desire to keep Roderigo's money coming in which causes him to hatch the plot against the couple and then Cassio. Iago's web of deceit and destructive intentions grow, as the play progresses, until we are not quite sure what his final or main aim is, or whether he knows himself.

Bradley says Iago has a general 'spite against goodness in men', so while any virtue exists he attempts to eliminate it. It is as if he is suffering from a disease or addiction, or controlled by an external force, and his appetite for sadistic enjoyment and power grows by what it feeds on. Hazlitt claimed that Iago destroys himself, since he 'is himself the dupe and victim of his ruling passion — an insatiable craving after action of the most difficult and dangerous kind'. Other critics point to the bungled attempt on Cassio's life as the turning point for Iago's successes, but even Emilia's and Bianca's arrivals on the scene are handled by Iago without suspicion falling on himself, and Emilia fails to prevent the murder of Desdemona and therefore Othello's suicide. It is true that Cassio is not supposed to survive, that Emilia's death may not have been intended, and that Roderigo's taking a long time to die is unfortunate for Iago. However, his refusal to speak at the end still leaves him in a position of control, something he seems to value more than anything else, and therefore he cannot categorically be said to have failed.

Iago the alien
Some critics and directors have seen Iago as a victim of 'otherness'. His problem could take the form of feeling inferior in his home city-state because of the upper-class milieu he is moving in, and of his having been rejected as Othello's number two by the preference for Cassio. All the other male characters in the play outrank Iago, are of higher social status, and have greater wealth or education. He is the black sheep and resists this state of affairs by turning everyone else black rather than allowing them to feel superior in their whiteness, and by showing them that their whiteness is in any case fraudulent because they are no more moral, civilised or

successful than he is, and, in fact, less so. What he proves indubitably is that he is much cleverer. His failure to become lieutenant could have triggered rage against the unfairness of a military system which rewards theory over practice and social graces over loyal soldiering. If he cannot belong to the club, he may feel the desire to pull down the pillars supporting it, which are noble birth, piety and land ownership. Venice could be seen as having betrayed him by letting a woman he could never hope to aspire to marry a black man, and by allowing his coveted position to go to a Florentine. He is in many ways the odd one out and this is shown by his colloquial language and silent stage presences. His soliloquies reveal that he has many grievances of 'otherness' — whilst claiming to represent the norm — and therefore many reasons to behave in the vengeful way that he does.

The many faces of Iago

Reams have been written over the centuries on how Iago should be regarded and what he represents, and directors/actors have tried a multitude of ways of presenting him, including some quite extreme ones. He has been described by most adjectives you care to name, many of them mutually exclusive, which is unusual for a literary character. The many possible interpretations of Iago's character and role can be combined into groups under headings, but some of these appear to be incompatible, which confirms the themes of paradox and doubleness in the play. When you have decided which view of Iago you find most convincing, it would be useful for you to collect evidence from the text in the form of quotations by and about him, and examples of events and incidents to support your case. You could use the following headings:

- the director
- the opportunist
- the Prince of Darkness
- the pragmatist
- the misanthropist
- the revolutionary

Iago's soliloquies

In Shakespeare's plays there is usually empathy between the audience and the characters who speak alone on stage, even the villainous ones. The dramatic device of the soliloquy gives us the speaker's perspective and makes us, in part, his accomplices, as we are taken into his confidence and listen to his plots being hatched against the other characters. Iago speaks to the audience throughout the play, unlike Othello, and thus draws us into his web. The theatrical convention is that in soliloquy the character tells the truth, but Iago may be an exception in that he may not know himself what the truth is about his own feelings. Coleridge claimed that Iago's soliloquies are 'the motive-hunting of motiveless malignity'.

Iago's soliloquies are an integral part of the plot structure in that they tend to fall at the beginning or end of scenes, where they either preview what is about to happen, or summarise and reflect back on what has just happened and the response of the others. This strategic placing of the speeches gives the impression that Iago is playing the role of chorus in a play of his own devising, and that he is the source of all the action. His soliloquies repay close attention for the wealth of material they provide for a discussion of the characters, themes and imagery of the play, as well as for what they reveal of the audacity of his own mind.

A study of the language and arguments of the seven soliloquies seems to reveal aspects of Iago's character. However, some of his alleged attitudes are contradicted elsewhere, and it is difficult to separate the true from the false, or to arrive at any overall interpretation of his motivation, which is why Coleridge was puzzled. One has to assume that this was deliberate and a stroke of genius on Shakespeare's part, since by making Iago's villainy so irrational and unfathomable he created one of his most memorable and terrifying characters. The seven soliloquies can be found in:

- Act I scene 3 (lines 377–98)
- Act II scene 1 (lines 277–303)
- Act II scene 3 (lines 44–59)
- Act II scene 3 (lines 326–52 and 371–77)
- Act III scene 3 (lines 316–26)
- Act IV scene 1 (lines 93–103)
- Act V scene 1 (lines 11–22)

The art of persuasion

In Act III scene 3 Othello is persuaded within 150 lines not only to doubt his wife's fidelity but to have her spied upon; within another 240 lines he has bonded himself to Iago, and a few minutes later he has sworn to murder Desdemona the same evening. The number and range of persuasive devices employed by Iago, both in choice of words and types of strategy, combined with the over-active imagination and insecurities of Othello, make this less surprising than many critics have claimed. Iago appeals to Othello's logic and rationality, while actually manipulating him psychologically and emotionally, until he creates a dependency in Othello. Othello believes that Iago is sympathetic to his cause, and when Iago swears to do anything Othello asks of him to show his support, Othello allows Iago to replace Desdemona in his esteem and affection, and as his confidant and soulmate.

The skills and advantages which enable Iago to be so successful in what critics call the 'temptation scene' are the Satanic powers of both linguistic and psycho-logical manipulation. The sheer weight of words also needs to be taken into account, since Iago has 90 lines to Othello's 60, giving him the upper hand in the dialogue in which the content and reactions are determined by Iago and have been planned by him in advance. Iago has fluency of expression and of ideas, a slickness of tongue and mind, and a skill of insinuation such that what is implied cannot be disproved nor held to his account. As an actor he also has confidence in delivery, the ability to put on a mask, and the gift of improvisation to enable him to take advantage of any opportunity. In addition, Iago is a soldier who knows from experience when to feint a retreat in order to advance further.

Legal strategy

Iago's tactics and intentions are collectively to imply some hidden unpleasantness, to put a different complexion on something to make it seem less innocent, or to present a hypothesis as if it were fact. Juries cannot strike things from their mind, though judges may order them to do so, and what's said cannot be unsaid. At the same time Iago disclaims any responsibility for the reliability of his information and pretends not necessarily to believe it himself, so that he can appear innocent of malicious intent and force Othello into the role of accuser. He builds up a case against Desdemona and Cassio from purely circumstantial evidence.

He is most fittingly described as ***advocatus diaboli***, the devil's advocate. He chooses phrases judiciously to have maximum visual effect in Othello's mind and yet simultaneously to appear to be concrete, objective, and 'probal to thinking' (II.3.328), such as the repeated use of 'other proofs' — which do not actually exist. He creates unbearable tension and suspense through delaying giving answers, which not only makes Othello more desperate for information ('Would I were satisfied!' III.3.387), but more likely to credit it when he does get it. To use a phrase of William Blake's, 'he publishes doubt and calls it knowledge'. Ironically, doubt is the basis of the adversarial judicial system, and although the aim of the law is to appeal to reason and to establish the truth, it is a lawyer's job to disguise doubt as knowledge and to influence the jury by the use of rhetoric and emotive language.

Power of words

Iago demonstrates more noticeably and concentratedly in Acts III and IV what he does throughout the play: he degrades people, relationships, values, facts and language. By putting words into new contexts and in a doubtful tone of voice, he calls into question the possibility of certainty. The verb 'think', which should mean a rational activity, in Iago's vocabulary comes to mean something which is vague, subjective and unprovable, which then casts doubt on Desdemona and Cassio's 'honesty'. Words are the link between unexpressed thoughts and irrevocable actions, and by controlling words Iago controls everything.

Iago's persuasive devices lead the 'ass' Othello through a sequence of emotional stages in the 'temptation scene', starting at III.3.90 when Desdemona leaves a love-struck Othello who is apprehensive about what would happen if he should lose her. Iago then plays Othello like a musical instrument through the full range of his notes: puzzlement, curiosity, anxiety, fear, frustration, anger, self-righteousness, conviction. Iago's most frequently repeated words in Act III are: 'kiss', 'honesty', 'bed', 'foolish', 'man'. These turn abstract love into physical sex, which by extension and implication inevitably lead a fool who thought his wife was honest to the real-isation and visualisation of his wife in bed with and being kissed by another man. Repetition is an insistent refrain which works on the brain of the recipient who is defenceless if the device is not consciously perceived (compare the brainwashing of Roderigo in Act I scene 3). It is worth analysing and collecting examples of the persuasive techniques which Iago employs between III.3.35 and IV.1.211. Quite often a single line contains examples of more than one technique, such is his verbal dexterity.

Iago's defence

In some ways Iago is a 'black' Hamlet (intelligent, observant, sceptical, frustrated, conscious of hypocrisy and self-serving in his fellow men, questioning what it is to be human, with a sense of humour, sarcasm and irony). Yet whereas Hamlet finally acquiesces in his heaven-ordained destiny and recognises that there is a divine order and a limit to human understanding, Iago, like Satan, chooses the other path, out of pride, which is to refuse to accept his position in the scheme of things and to ally himself with evil to prove that there is no such thing as good. However, it is easier for princes and generals to see a divine plan in the social hierarchy than for bastard sons (for example Edmund in *King Lear*) and ensigns, and Iago could be seen as the spirit of democracy or socialism reacting against and trying to overturn a corrupt system of privilege and complacency. If he is, as he claims, a previous and continuing victim of jealousy, 'a monster/Begot upon itself' (III.4.157–58), then perhaps he should attract as much sympathy as Othello. Emilia confirms that someone 'turned your wit the seamy side without' (IV.2.145), revealing the ugly side which was not meant to show, like white turning black, and perhaps the former Iago was a much pleasanter person. Iago may be a victim of class prejudice, deprived of any beauty in his life, and since the bullied become bullies in their turn, he may be passing on his own unjust suffering.

No comment

Iago refuses to show repentance at the end of the play. His last words are 'Demand me nothing; what you know, you know:/From this time forth I never will speak word.' He regrets nothing, so there is nothing to say. He recognises there are no satisfactory explanations or mitigating circumstances for what he has done, nor words to put it into; or else he believes the characters did it to themselves, were asking for it, and therefore he has nothing to feel guilty about and they do not deserve an explanation. He does not accept their right to ask or to judge and punish him. As the *Penguin* introduction puts it, 'Iago believes in nothing, least of all in other human beings.' His defiant stance is consistent with his first words in the play, and shows that Iago has not changed at all. He despises emotion, self-pity, weakness and subordination, so refuses to affect any of them and conveys an inhuman self-command which frightens the audience as well as the remaining characters. It is a final act of torture to withhold the knowledge of himself which might help them to understand what has happened to them.

It is a rule of tragedy that 'nothing is in doubt and everyone's destiny is known' in the final moments, but at the end of *Othello*, Iago is still alive and defiant, unlike the villains in Shakespeare's other major tragedies, and we must ask ourselves why Shakespeare allows Iago to live. The audience cannot feel absolutely confident that Iago will receive his just deserts, because of the vagueness of the stipulated punishment, because we doubt Cassio's ruthlessness, and because we have reason to fear that Iago could easily out-talk his gaoler or outwit his torturers and escape. Being sentenced to torture, however, might be considered a worse punishment than instant death, and a fitting poetic justice for his crime. Ironically, Venetian law protects Iago, since no one can simply kill him with impunity, not even Desdemona's relatives, however much they feel they'd like to or that he deserves it.

Symbolically, Iago can represent, like the perpetual barbarian threat, an invincible force for evil which can be temporarily defeated but never exterminated — 'I bleed, sir, but not killed' (V.2.285) — and which will live to fight another day. Othello is by all accounts an efficient killer and manages to despatch himself a few lines later with no trouble, but he is unable to kill Iago, following the utterance 'If that thou be'st a devil, I cannot kill thee'. This rather reinforces the idea that he is a supernatural being who leads a charmed life.

The three women

Women's parts in plays did not equal men's in number, size or status because they were written for boy actors with unbroken voices, since it was unacceptable for women to perform in public. However, Shakespeare was famously interested in female perspectives and psychology, and women have significant roles in all the major tragedies as wives and daughters. None of them live to the end of their respective plays.

Ownership

A woman's place was in the home and she had no role to play in the public arena. Women were possessions and dependent on their fathers until they were handed over to the rule of their husbands, whom they also had to love, honour and obey. Since females were considered to be naturally inferior in intellect and morality, their feelings or points of view were not considered; all decisions were taken for them and they were expected to accept them without argument and carry out the wishes of men. They had no education and, as Othello describes, their job was to be 'delicate with a needle' and 'sing the savageness out of a bear'. The consequences of not performing these daughterly and wifely duties were serious, involving being disowned and deprived of a home, financial support and a place in society; prostitution was often the only way to survive without a dowry or supportive male relative. Othello's first reaction to Desdemona's alleged infidelity is to say he will 'whistle her off…to prey at fortune'. Women could only rise through their association with men and their rank, hence Emilia's assertion that she would commit adultery if it meant making Iago a monarch.

For women, male ownership meant being subjected to restriction of movement and lack of control over their bodies; Brabantio asks 'How got she out?' (I.1.170) and Othello is determined not to allow Desdemona's body to be used by other men. It was a man's worst nightmare to have a wife or daughter who caused a loss of his honour and status in the community through attracting gossip and besmirching her reputation. Othello laments 'That we can call these delicate creatures ours/And not their appetites' (III.3.266–67). If they feel they do not have control of their possessed female's sexuality, they have to disown it (Brabantio) or kill it (Othello) or punish them for it (Iago), even though it is something the women can do nothing about because the fear of their promiscuity lies in the heads of the men. Judging from Iago's suspicions of Emilia with both Cassio and Othello, any sound-bodied male who could be considered in some way superior to themselves in looks or status is suspected with their nightcap.

Though they seem to represent three social levels, the women in the play all accept that they are powerless and subject to male decree and patronage; Emilia has no choice but to accompany the party to Cyprus, as Othello has ordered it, and Desdemona could not have stayed in Venice, having been cast out by her father. Desdemona wants a different life from the one she was born to and her father had in mind for her, but she has no more real control over her life than Bianca, who accepts her fate with the line 'I must be circumstanced' (III.4.197).

Double standards

Social attitudes to male and female sexual behaviour then, as now, were very different: male promiscuity, adultery, pre- or extra-marital sex were not condemned and were considered natural. Cassio's consorting with a prostitute, whether married or not, would be a commonplace and not only expected of men generally — and soldiers in particular — but even admired. Roderigo's death is a punishment for his foolishness, not for his 'unlawful solicitation' of a married woman, which was licensed by medieval romantic literature. By contrast, fornicating women were considered a threat to the church and to the fabric of society; they were blamed for leading men astray, destroying men's honour and bringing shame on the extended family. Women were thought to be easily seduced, being descended from Eve, betrayer of mankind.

Critics have commented on the dislocation of love and sex the men in the play share, but which does not affect the women. Men wished to marry virgins and to have chaste wives for social reasons, but have whores available for their pleasure, thereby creating the dichotomy of the two types of women, reputable and not. Women's social position was determined by their relationship to men and consequent sexual status; there were only four categories (with no equivalent male versions): maiden; wife; widow; whore. A fifth category — witch — was reserved for those not regarded as real women because of their masculine characteristics, ugliness or barrenness (see *Macbeth*). Any non-conformist and manless woman was likely, until the late seventeenth century, to be accused of witchcraft (42 'witches' were burned in 1570) and of sexual congress with the devil. James I wrote a book in 1597 called *Daemonologie* — such was his fascination with witches — and he held witch trials famous for their unfairness, whereby it was impossible for the accused, like Desdemona, to prove her innocence.

Two key words relating to conflict in the play are 'nature' and 'freedom'. These words have different values and connotations depending on gender, and in particular are problematic when applied to Desdemona. She wants her freedom in eloping with the Moor, but he is giving up his in putting 'into circumscription and confine' his 'unhoused free condition' (I.2.26–27). Her freedom of action and of speech is seen as being too free by some of the men and, for a woman of her rank, her behaviour and choices can be seen as unnatural, i.e. not sufficiently socially conditioned and controlled.

Reputation, reputation, reputation

What distinguishes a respectable married woman like Emilia from a 'strumpet' like Bianca is not her appearance or social background, or even her sexual behaviour, but her reputation, i.e. the label she is given by society. This made reputation an essential commodity for social survival, yet it was vulnerable to attack by any dissatisfied male. There was no forum in which calumny could be contested (one cannot prove a negative, i.e. that one is not a woman of loose morals; see *Measure for Measure*) and a reputation once lost could not be regained. The fallen woman became the prey of gossips, and was ostracised and excluded from polite society, necessitating suicide or entrance into a nunnery.

A combination of the prejudices of the church against disobedient Eve, stereo-types from classical literature of treacherous and faithless women, and the medieval icon of Fortune as a female arbitrarily turning her wheel, had all gained women the reputation of being untrustworthy and inconstant. As Hamlet puts it in his accusation against his mother, girlfriend and all women, 'Frailty, thy name is woman'. Iago despises not only women but what he perceives as feminine charac-teristics in Othello and Cassio, which betray militarism and masculinity; he himself stands for constancy, practicality, and everything else unfeminine.

Silent victims

The virgin, newly-wed or demure widow was a target for predatory rakes and lechers whose conquest of the apparently unattainable was an irresistible challenge to their masculinity, and brides and betrothed women, being in a state of transition, were particularly vulnerable to assault and slander. Though the men were rarely punished, in reality or fiction, the conquered literary female had to die or be killed. Desdemona seems doomed at birth by her name, meaning 'unfortunate'.

It is interesting that characters and audiences alike are concerned at the injustice of Desdemona's death on the grounds that she was not guilty, not because it would be unacceptable for her to be murdered even if she had slept with Cassio. Christ refused to condemn the woman taken in adultery, yet Othello, claiming to be a devout Christian, takes the law, and role of God, into his own hands. In this trial of Desdemona — in absentia, on a charge of fornication, in an all-male court — there are counsel and witness for the prosecution, and a suborned judge, but no counsel for the defence. She is guilty whether she accepts the verdict or disputes it, damned if she does and damned if she doesn't.

Women were expected to be seen but not heard, even or especially in their husbands' or fathers' presence. In the Middle Ages punishments were designed specifically for scolding and nagging wives. Together Emilia, with 245 lines, and Desdemona, with 388, only have half as many as Iago. They were not only expected to speak only when invited to, i.e. rarely, but to be absent if their 'owner' desired it: all three women are told to go away in Act III, and all three women in the play endanger their life, and two of them lose it, for daring to break silence, and either do not get to present their case or are punished for doing so. Desdemona is disowned as much for daring to defend herself to the Senate as she is for her shocking marriage.

Between them the women show the passive and subordinate position of women in Venetian society, who must wait to be visited, proposed to and sent for. They cannot be thinkers, performers or advisers, and must content themselves with following the instructions of and trying to please their elders and betters. Though they may have temper tantrums (Bianca) or be critical of men in private (Emilia), essentially they have no choice but to conform and comply on pain of rejection, violence or death. Desdemona learns not to complain and, with the psychology of the victim of domestic violence, begins to blame herself and make excuses for her abuser.

Male fantasies

In medieval and sixteenth-century literature, written by men, women tended to be represented as either Christian martyrs or malevolent devils, one extreme or the other (and this continued until the end of the nineteenth century). Characters divide women into virgins and saints or whores and devils, with nothing in between; the former could become the latter overnight, but not vice versa. Women, as the unknowable 'other', could easily be seen as the enemy and destroyer, pretending to be angels, but really in league with Satan to lure men to their doom through seduction and enchantment. Men were afraid of female beauty because it gave women a kind of magical power over them which could not be resisted with logic. Iago's attack on women in II.1.145–57 is not just his own; he is giving a catalogue of well-known criticisms of women, as indicated by the rhyming couplets. Dialogues between all the male characters reveal a deep-seated fear of women deceiving them and thereby gaining supremacy and making them a laughing-stock, as also revealed by Brabantio's dream, Cassio's reaction to the idea that Bianca wants him to marry her, and Othello's horror of cuckoldry.

The male characters all desire or worship Desdemona, putting her on a pedestal from which she will inevitably fall when she is not able to live up to the male ideals of perfection and divinity. The one female dialogue in the play shows that women are at the mercy of men and their fantasies, and Desdemona asks Othello 'What horrible fancy's this?' (IV.2.25). Women are texts for men to look at and interpret, and they have no protection against extreme readings and unfair judgements, but yet they cannot refuse to be assessed, as Shakespeare shows in his next play (*King Lear*) with Cordelia. Women cannot win, however they play the game: Desdemona's forwardness when Othello comes to visit and her willingness to sacrifice reputation, family name and her father's love to pursue her desire for an exotic stranger gives ammunition to those who want to claim there is something of the slut in her, though they are also what prove her love. It is her very purity and innocence that make Roderigo and Iago lust after her, but these qualities make her their unwitting and helpless prey.

Desdemona

Desdemona is a Christian martyr who is pure, chaste, devoted to her earthly and heavenly lord and master, and who has the virtues of faith, hope and charity. She is associated with light, which is divine but vulnerable. She is very young, and the verbal chastisement, physical punishment and withdrawal of love she suffers put her in the position of an abused child. Her role is to be sacrificed on an altar to redeem mankind, though her domestic duties are more mundane, and she can only listen to romantic tales by slipping away from the household chores. Being motherless, she is a literary stereotype which also reflects the social reality that huge numbers of women died in childbirth then (and until the late nineteenth century). Like Cinderella or a fairy-tale princess locked in a castle by an ogre, she is waiting for her prince to rescue her and carry her off to an exciting new life. She is forced to deceive her father in order to win her freedom, but she is naïve in choosing Othello; exogamy, marrying outside one's race and community, was not something to be done casually at that time (unless, like Shylock's daughter, she has deliberately chosen the husband least acceptable to her domineering father in order to spite him). She is also naïve about marriage, refusing to believe that unfaithful wives exist and there is doubt about how well she really knows and understands her husband.

Emilia

Emilia has the worldliness and resignation of her station as a servant and the desperation of the childless, unloved wife. She gets caught by the demands of her husband and is forced to lie, but finally chooses good over evil when it is too late. She conveys the gender inequalities within marriage and in conventional public behaviour, and represents the stereotype of the dismissed, silenced woman who finally fights back, but is killed by the patriarchal system for her temerity in doing so. She is a surrogate mother figure to Desdemona as well as a maid, with all the ironies this involves.

Bianca

As a courtesan who falls in love with a client, she reflects the paradox of Venetian sexual morality. As a sexual mercenary, she could be said to ply a 'trade' for profit in the same way as the men of war do, yet is treated very differently. She could never expect to marry, or even be believed, because her sexual status is seen as indicative of her general moral character. She causes Cassio to reveal himself to be of dubious integrity in not wanting Othello to see him 'womaned', and it is ironic that she is disapproved of and accused of dishonesty by Emilia and Iago.

Missing women

Leaving aside Cassio's ambiguous 'fair wife' (I.1.21), the absent women referred to in the play are: Brabantio's wife/Desdemona's mother; Othello's mother; Desdemona's mother's maid, Barbary; and the rejected woman of the Willow Song. These ghostly women's stories and situations make up another group of silent female victims, who are betrayed, killed by childbirth or a broken heart, or live in fear of losing their man's love. They remind the audience that the fates of the women in the play are typical and traditional, rather than extraordinary.

Venice and Cyprus

Act I of *Othello* is set in Venice, but the following four acts take place in Cyprus. The two locations in the play are mentioned many times, and they are not only integral to the plot but intrinsic to its characterisation and themes. As Shakespeare and his audiences must have known, Cyprus was definitively taken by the Turks a few months after the setting of the play in 1570, which adds the extra irony that the Venetian republic has only temporarily averted the barbarian threat.

Super-subtle Venetians

In 1600 Venice was approximately the same size as London and had many foreign residents and visitors because of trade links with the East and north Africa. It was not only powerful and respected by eastern and western nations but a by-word for beauty, culture and civilisation. However, it was also thought of as a pleasure capital and known for its sexual tolerance and celebrated courtesans (the 'cunning whore[s] of Venice' of whom Othello is aware). The Senate, however dignified, is engaged in war for profit and territory, and Othello and Cassio are mercenaries, killing for hire. There is other evidence of the corruption caused by imperial ambition, wealth and complacency in Brabantio's imprisonment of his daughter for the purpose of arranging a good marriage, and Roderigo's 'unlawful solicitation' of Desdemona through the use of his money as bribes. Iago has also made money his replacement for morality, having hired 'three great ones of the city' to plead his suit for the lieutenancy — a position obviously not expected to be awarded on merit — and being a confidence trickster and pimp for financial gain. Venice is therefore a less virtuous place than it might appear, which sets the keynote for the play, and the 'super-subtle' Venetians do not invite much respect, all being obsessed with money and trading in human flesh, including Emilia — who thinks that adultery can be condoned if the price is right — and the ironically named Bianca, who sells her body for nice clothes.

In addition, the racism in the play is expressed by four Venetian characters: Iago, Roderigo, Brabantio and Emilia. When faced with something which cannot be understood rationally, because 'unnatural', a leading senator of the Venetian state falls back on the accusation of witchcraft; the veneer of civilisation is thin, and prejudice and superstition lurk just beneath the surface. This contributes to the play's theme of appearance versus reality, and to the idea that underneath the visible white surface lies blackness.

The baseness of Venice is revealed in the opening of the play with the shouting of obscenities in the public street and the connection of sex with money and control. Othello and Desdemona's love could be viewed as already contaminated, making the degradation which follows seem inevitable if even Desdemona's innocence is infected by the wealthy city. It may be significant that the only winner in the play is Cassio, who is specifically distinguished from the others as a Florentine.

Warlike isle

The location, history and atmosphere of Cyprus, where the tragic events occur, are significant to the themes of the play. Described twice in Act II as 'this war-like isle', Cyprus is apparently the antithesis to peaceful Venice. Less well fortified than Rhodes, it is more vulnerable to the traditional Venetian enemy, the Moslem barbarian. Having always been a colony, Cyprus has never had autonomy, and is therefore a symbol of submission. Since it was thought to be the birthplace of Aphrodite, goddess of love, it is an island of love dominated by war. As the last European bastion against the marauding infidel it is isolated, occupied, under threat and in a state of turbulence, with its people dependent and frightened. This is the mental state Othello falls into after his arrival there, thanks to the machinations of the 'Turk' Iago, who invades, captures and then subjects him to his rule. As the battlefield between the forces of Christianity and heathenism, Cyprus represents actual war and also the figurative thematic battles between good and evil, light and darkness, heaven and hell. It hosts two street fights, drunkenness, prostitution, murder, verbal and physical attacks on women, and a general loss of decorum and normality indicative of chaos, as if the transition from Venice to Cyprus has unlocked the primitive side of previously restrained characters, including Othello. Not one of the major characters returns from Cyprus to Venice within the play, as if it is not a journey which can be made in reverse, like loss of virginity, reputation, trust and innocence. Cyprus is where European meets Turk and loses the battle of civilisation and humanity.

The Moor of Venice

Othello is a Moor employed by Venice who is sent to Cyprus and does not return; one can see a parallel between his movements and the development of his character. Othello presents his past as a romantic and exotic tale of heroic exploits, but it is essentially no more than superstition and barbarism retold in the grand style to disguise the bloody brutality of hand-to-hand combat (which is shown to be damaging to one's humanity in *Macbeth*). During his 9 months in Venice, where he is a double outsider — being black and a recent arrival — Othello has reinvented himself as a public figure: confident, entertaining and, most of all, Christian. He has exchanged freedom and the hard couch of the 'tented field' for the 'soft couch' of Venus.

In Cyprus there is no visible enemy and Othello loses his 'occupation', which is his military career and the excitement suggestive of battle. The sophisticated veneer is peeled away by Iago, and Othello seems to revert to a former self brought up by Moorish parents to believe in magic handkerchiefs, love as a kind of spell and religion as superstition. The savage still lurks beneath the honorary white man, and as he loses confidence in his assumed identity because of the effect of Cyprus and the undermining influence of Iago, he starts to see himself as his detractors see him: black, old and uncivilised (III.3.260–64). Another Othello now emerges, the Moslem Moor and brother of the heathen Turk, enemy of the state and of peace, the irrational murdering force which is the inner correlative of the external war threat. The only way harmony can be restored is for this awakening and uprising to be suppressed; one Othello kills the other at the end, an act more of battle than of suicide, when once again the public imposes on the private.

The infidel

We can also interpret Iago's behaviour in terms of the move from Venice to Cyprus. The seeds sown in Cyprus, however fertile the ground, were engendered in the Venice of double standards. Taking his 'dog' Roderigo with him, Iago sets up his own empire in Cyprus, arriving before Othello with Desdemona already firmly in tow. He knows everyone and everything, and feels even more confident and less restricted than in Venice, where he is kept in his place.

At home in a war zone, Iago gives free rein to his own excesses and releases those of the hitherto courtly Cassio and demure Desdemona (who seems unable to see that she is behaving inappropriately in her championing of Cassio and criticism of Othello as a ditherer). Their losses, insecurities and communication breakdowns fuel his game plan and war stratagem. The convenient employment of his wife as Desdemona's maid gives him another avenue to exploit. Iago arrives in Cyprus in the guise of a protector, but parallels are quickly drawn between his actions and those of the diabolical infidel. He can be seen as carrying out the work of the Turk in creating chaos and destruction, undermining Christianity and the sanctity of marriage. However, he forfeits the ability to return to his homeland at the end, doomed to spend his remaining days in the prison which Cyprus becomes for him.

Time and speed

Although a relatively short play, *Othello* subjects the audience to intense and pro-longed dramatic tension because of its tightly-wound structure. There are no changes of perspective, sub- or parallel plots, or memorable comic interludes with fools, porters, gravediggers and such like, as there are in the other major tragedies, and the audience is particularly conscious of the chain of cause and effect driving the play.

Double time scheme

Othello is often referred to as having a double time scheme; this means that some events could only realistically take place in 'long time', that is over a period of weeks or even months, whereas others are placed in a context of 'short time', happening within a few hours of each other with specific time references attached. Acts II–V cover only 33 hours and the whole play seems to be condensed into a matter of days.

The voyage to Cyprus from Venice by the main characters would have taken several weeks, depending on the winds, and Cassio says that Iago and Desdemona have arrived a week earlier than expected. Gratiano and Lodovico also travel to Cyprus with a new commission for Othello, after receiving news that the Turkish fleet has been destroyed, both of which which would have taken time. Allusions which suggest that a significant period of time has passed are Emilia saying that her husband has asked her 'a hundred times' to steal the handkerchief; Bianca accusing Cassio of having not visited her for 8 days; Othello claiming that Desdemona and Cassio have committed 'the act of shame/A thousand times' (V.2.211); Roderigo lamenting that he has spent in Cyprus all the money from the sale of his land in Venice, while waiting 'every day' in vain for some response from Desdemona to his suit and his gift of jewels. On the other hand, there are specific time references which indicate that only one full night and one full day are spent in Cyprus before the end of the play. The double time scheme gives the play the advantages of both long and short time: plausibility of psychology and event, as well as an alarming pace and sudden shocking contrasts. 'We must obey the time' says Othello in I.3.297, making himself subservient to it, as he does to Iago.

Night-time

Most of the action of the play takes place at night. Under cover of darkness people reveal the unacceptable facets of their character to the audience; however, these remain unperceived by the characters in the play, as is the case with Iago and Roderigo. A different and less attractive side to Cassio emerges during the hours of darkness. It is difficult to see, recognise or be sure of anything without sufficient light — this is demonstrated by the characters' need to be told the identity of each other in the street scenes. Iago lurks in and thrives on darkness, the element of hell. The play begins and ends at night, suggesting that the battle between good and evil is incontestably won by the forces of darkness. Desdemona is associated with fairness, love and truth, and is doomed, by the play's insistence on black, to be as extin-guishable as a tiny star in a dark firmament of male machination and exploitation (all five male characters have designs of some kind on Desdemona). The atmosphere of war casts a dark shadow. Chaos is represented by the coming of night and putting out of the light.

Alarming speed

Time runs too fast from the beginning of the play, interrupting hours of love with the urgency of war and not allowing anything to be completed. At the end, Emilia arrives just too late to save her mistress, reminding us of our human limitations and suggesting that a greater power is in charge of events and outcomes. The pace of the play isolates the characters and deprives them of the opportunity for commu-nication. When the play starts, an event has occurred which is already too late to reverse — and which may have been impetuous — and it seems as though the marriage has started a swift chain of cause and effect which pulls in everyone else. The audience is swept along by the chronological logic of the sequence of events, but the pace makes us feel uncomfortable.

Iago's soliloquies contribute to the feeling of speed by their content, structure and positioning. 'Dull not device by coldness and delay' (II.3.377) he says, the quick-thinker and improviser whose mind is seen to be working at an alarming rate. He can cover several hatreds, plans and comments on humanity's failings in a few lines, seeming to be not only reacting to the quick succession of events but also creating them. He is able to give the impression that time and speed are on his side (Iago congratulates himself that 'My boat sails freely both with wind and stream' (II.3.59)), that he is their agent or vice versa. This lends him an aura of supernatural power, loading the dice against Othello and Desdemona. Because the soliloquies comment on an action just completed and also immediately set up the next one, they seem to be the link and driving force of the plot, which is unfolding itself at breakneck speed. They are a stream of consciousness, putting thought into words and words into deeds with no respite or pause for consideration.

Quick change

Othello changes from a doting husband ('But I do love thee!' III.3.91) to a lamenting one ('Why did I marry?' III.3.240) without a scene break. That jealousy can strike and claim a victim in 150 lines, or about 20 minutes, demonstrates the overwhelming power of an emotion against which humans are helpless and reason is impotent (another example is *The Winter's Tale*, in which Leontes is overcome within a few seconds without any persuasion). Furthermore, it is proof of Iago's power that he can cause a newly-married man in love to want to murder his wife in such a short time.

The absence of a scene break means the pressure can be applied to Othello relentlessly, and dramatic tension is kept up for the audience. It simultaneously makes the speed of his change shockingly fast but also more credible, because he has no time for reflection; he is not given a chance to sleep on it and talk with Desdemona, but is carried along on the tide of Iago's insinuations and rhetoric. Iago puts on a sustained and impressive performance to parallel that of Satan tempting and seducing Eve with the apple of knowledge, which also supposedly happened in a few minutes. We are not wholly surprised by the speed of Othello's change, as we have already witnessed the power of language to change Desdemona (Othello's storytelling made her behave impulsively and apparently out of character) and Roderigo (who has been put under Iago's spell with the use of similar linguistic and psychological methods).

Love and war

In the medieval period of chivalry, the courtly lover was a knight dedicated to a cause and devoted to his lady, whose favour he won through his military skills and dangerous quests, as well as by being handsome and attentive. In *Othello*, the three main male characters are soldiers, but the three women want to be loved.

True love?

The various types of love exemplified in the play are all questionable. Brabantio's love for his daughter seems more like possessiveness, and he is quick to disown and repudiate her; his dying of 'pure grief' may be a consequence of his loss of respect in Venetian society because of his daughter's 'match' and his shame at the prospect of 'filthy' progeny. Desdemona does not seem unduly worried to have lost her father's love and does not express her feelings towards him, except in the one comment 'I have lost him too' (IV.2.46). Self-love, the primary sin of pride, could be laid at Iago's door, and possibly Othello's. Roderigo is in the grip of infatuation, an obsessive but illusory form of love which can depart as quickly as it arrives, and apparently does so in his case. For Iago, romantic love does not exist, being 'merely a lust of the blood' and 'a permission of the will' (I.3.331), and this seems to describe not only his own marriage but also Cassio's relationship with Bianca. Iago dishonestly avows his love for Othello, in the ancient and feudal traditions of dutiful affection between master and servant and brothers-in-arms. Emilia is willing to lie for her husband and die for her mistress (despite having known her for only a matter of days — see 'Time and Speed', pp. 60–62), but both of these forms of love seem adulterated by impure motives — self-interest and guilt respectively. For Othello, love is related to one's immortal soul and is expressed in heavy rhetoric and heavenly imagery, but this doesn't enable it to survive the first test. Desdemona's love does, but it is mixed with duty and the fear of being cast off again, and the audience wonders how much her vision of Othello is distorted by an unworldly and romantic lens.

Husband versus soldier

Othello embodies the conflict between the roles of husband and soldier, which is not a problem for Iago, since he does not believe in love or respect women. Othello is the antithesis of Cassio, an experienced soldier but an inexperienced lover. Othello is used to 'the flinty and steel couch of war' (I.3.228), has an affinity for 'hardness' (I.3.85), and his epithet in Act I is 'valiant'. He admits that he is 'little blessed with the soft phrase of peace' (I.3.82) and we never see him engaged in the gentle art of love. Only by chance encounter and Desdemona's encouragement does he become a lover during his 9 months' leave in Venice; he is there and invited into ruling-class homes because of his military expertise and experiences. Othello is not an independent being, but at the mercy of and a servant to the state, to be posted according to the Senate's will. An all-male environment and a soldier's lifestyle do not easily accommodate females and domesticity. The threat of war creates a background of pressing urgency which overrules the complaint of a bereft father and pushes all personal considerations aside, even on a husband's wedding night: the Duke tells Othello he must be 'content to slubber the gloss of your new fortunes with this more stubborn and boisterous expedition' (I.3.224–25).

Othello is described as 'the warlike Moor' prior to his arrival in Cyprus, a few lines before being identified with the 'warlike isle', and having battled with the 'dangerous sea', as if to stress the ascendance of the fighter over the lover. Love is disrupted from beginning to end by conflict and anger: 'tis the soldier's life/To have their balmy slumbers waked with strife' (II.3.250–51). Calling Desdemona his 'fair warrior' is a paradoxical phrase which draws attention to the two opposing demands on him which he must try to reconcile; the first night is a celebration of both the nuptials and the Turkish defeat. His masculinity and military authority are compromised when he shows tenderness to Desdemona in public at the harbour, which disgusts Iago and spurs him to action. It was his dramatic and fantastic tales of war which wooed the romantic Desdemona, and their relationship is therefore built on his soldierly past rather than on his potential for making a good husband.

When the Turk doesn't materialise externally, Othello is left without a professional role, and seems to turn on himself as a result. It is a bad sign when Othello rejects the music arranged by Cassio to celebrate their marriage and rises to check the fortifications instead. His military exploits define him, and without them he cannot prove who he is; he is only a Venetian while there is an identifiable enemy of the state. When he thinks he has lost his honour in marriage he says farewell to himself as a soldier (III.3.344–54). Othello is split in two and feels that only by killing his supposedly errant wife, and then himself, can he rediscover his former role of the crusader against evil. He has gained reputation and position in Venetian society through his military prowess; he loses all this through his marriage. His struggle with and slaughter of the enemy Desdemona seems like an attempt to undo the disastrous marital experiment.

Victors and victims

The Turkish threat of war symbolises not only the dark side of Othello, which will destroy him from within, but also Iago's determination to undermine marriage, society and the moral universe. Iago is a servant at the command of others, but unlike Othello he fights against the system and tries to prove he can defeat it through the strategic cunning and ruthlessness of the hardened campaigner. He is the spirit of competition and violence and he has the high ground throughout the play. He is too proud to be a suitor and despises the effete and effeminate Cassio, who cannot take his drink, talks poetic nonsense and kisses ladies' hands. Iago comments on the unmanliness of both Othello and Cassio, and despises women generically because they are not men and so cannot be soldiers. His triumph is to persuade Othello to confuse love and war in his feelings towards first Cassio and then Desdemona, and to make Othello and Roderigo think that disillusion and defeat can be turned into victorious conquest. He also tricks Roderigo into fatally exchanging the courtly lover's role in Venice for the assassin's cloak in Cyprus.

Desdemona is new to and naïve about both love and war, which for her are connected because of the idealism of her youth and the influence of romantic stories. She cannot differentiate between Othello as a husband and Othello as a soldier, not realising that she should not interfere in military matters. Neither can she seem to comprehend why Cassio cannot be immediately reinstated after his cashiering, without giving grave offence to the wounded Montano and to the Cypriots (whom he is there to protect from barbarism, rather than disturb with midnight brawls). She craves excitement and travel to compensate for her sheltered and restricted upbringing and to feed her imagination, and is determined not to be a 'moth of peace', but these desires lead her to her death.

Lieutenant Cassio is the link with the pre-play romantic and military events of the elopement and the promotion. He unites, as the uniformed lover, the comrade and the courtier, the public officer and the private womaniser. He worships the unattainable 'divine Desdemona' but wrangles with Bianca. Cassio is the subject of many comments and conversations between the main trio of characters about his swordplay and sexual prowess. As the only real survivor of the main characters, he is both victim and victor: Iago beat him, but is his to torture.

Private love and public war are interwoven and set at odds to create conflicts and ironies; the consummation of the marriage is interrupted twice by alarm calls, but conversely Othello and Desdemona's love causes a breach between family members, old colleagues and the Senate. The street brawls are provoked by love interests but are also a metaphor for the wars within the self and within relationships. Many speeches mix the language of the battlefield with the language of the bedroom, like Iago's in II.3.173–81 and in Act I scene 3 where he puns on Desdemona's 'provocation' and 'alarums'. The final scene is one of battlefield carnage on the bed of love. In all aspects of the play war wins over love, and therein lies the tragedy.

Jealousy and honesty

The green-eyed monster

Jealousy was considered to be an aspect of the deadly sin of envy, since both involve a desire to possess. The concept of jealousy had a wider meaning then than nowadays, but was most often used to denote suspicion of one's sexual partner. Many essay questions and discussions of *Othello* revolve around the extent to which Othello is guilty of jealousy, as it is traditionally considered to be the primary theme of the play. However, there are concerns about the sudden onset of Othello's jealousy. According to the Russian novelist Dostoevsky, 'Othello was not jealous, he was trustful', and Coleridge said: 'I do not think there is any jealousy, properly so called, in the character of Othello.' Othello, Desdemona and Iago ('The Moor is of a free and open nature') are at pains to point out that he is not jealous; certainly he has not so far shown any disposition to be so, having used Cassio as a chaperone and go-between, and having handed Desdemona over to Iago for the voyage to Cyprus. Coleridge asserts that 'Iago's suggestions…are quite new to him.' This may be true, and the reason they are so effective. One cannot protect oneself against something which cannot be foreseen and is outside one's previous experience.

There are other characters who might be considered to be guilty of jealousy or envy. Iago is envious of Cassio having the lieutenancy, good looks and manners, and a 'daily beauty in his life'; of Othello having Desdemona; and of Roderigo having money. He claims to believe that both Othello and Cassio have slept with his wife, Emilia, and convincingly describes sexual jealousy as a gnawing of the entrails. Bianca is jealous of the owner of the handkerchief, with whom she suspects Cassio has spent the last 8 days. Desdemona is envious of Othello's life of travel and excitement, and is determined to become a part of it, despite the unconventionality of her accompanying him to a war zone.

A matter of honour

The word 'honest' was in transition at the time *Othello* was written, according to the critic William Empson, and had several and, appropriately, almost opposite meanings: it denoted the aristocratic virtues of truthfulness, faithfulness and absence of duplicity — which is how it is mostly used in the play — but could also refer to a down-to-earth frankness and lack of pretension, which is how Iago sometimes makes ironic use of it. Its extensive usage in the play draws attention to it and gives rise to claims that it is honesty rather than jealousy which is the main theme. 'Honest' is used 52 times and 'honour' eight times; the two words are obviously related: without honesty, i.e. integrity, one can have no honour, that is respect and reputation. It is reputation which makes men 'immortal' (II.3.256) and the opposite of bestial, but because it is an abstract concept dependent on words spoken about someone, it is vulnerable to slander. The noble view, expressed by Cassio, was that death was preferable to dishonour.

There is evidence that Othello is as much or more concerned about his honour than about Desdemona's fidelity. His disastrous rejection of Cassio is caused by his belief that his honour has been impugned by Cassio's wounding of Montano. Coleridge claims that 'Iago would not have succeeded but by hinting that his honour was compromised.' The two are of course linked, since his imagined cuckoldry destroys his self-esteem, his standing in the eyes of other men and his position in society. Othello cannot bear the idea that he is keeping a corner in the thing he loves for others' use, or that others are laughing at him behind his back. At the time a man's honour was inseparable from his wife's behaviour and he was judged as much by how she was publicly perceived as by his own professional competence.

The fact that it is his friend and subordinate, Cassio, who is implicated is a key factor in Othello's mental torture. This means that he thinks he is being betrayed on sexual, personal and professional levels, and therefore suffers a triple attack on his honour. Iago manages to persuade Othello to side with the 'cause' of men against women, so that the final justification for the murder of Desdemona is the need to protect male honour generally: 'Yet she must die, else she'll betray more men' (V.2.6).

Because of the two possible meanings, 'honest, honest Iago' can be taken as a kind of pun. In the newer sense of open, in touch with natural desires, he could be called honest in that he describes and acts out the crude urges of human nature. By comparison with Cassio, Othello and Roderigo, he could also be perceived as being more manly — another sense of 'honest' — in that they put on airs and graces and use elaborate, courtly and poetic language, while Iago's speech is blunt. He despises the foppish affectations of Cassio and the slavery of Othello to the 'captain's captain', Desdemona, and thinks that they dishonour the profession of soldier.

'Honest' when applied to women meant chaste, faithful to one's husband, and Othello and Iago use it repeatedly in this sense. Desdemona is accused of the double dishonesty of lying and of lying with other men, as though one is a symptom of, and therefore evidence of, the other. As the *Penguin* introduction points out (p. 24), this is a drama of marital, parental and professional honour, while the national honour of Venice is also at stake. It would therefore not be difficult to argue that the theme of honour and honesty is at least as important as jealousy in the play, and one which has wider applications and implications.

Seeing and knowing

Though the characters in *Othello* construe everyone else's smiles, gestures and behaviour 'quite in the wrong' (IV.I.103), the audience is given the responsibility of interpreting them correctly. Nearly every scene in the play refers to or depends upon a character seeing and knowing something or someone.

Seeing is believing

Many Elizabethans believed that external appearance revealed inner reality, but Shakespeare was interested in exploring the problem of a fair exterior which conceals an inner foulness. His plays explore the issues of good and evil, truth and falsity, particularly in the major tragedies; *Othello* is asking how much one can ever know, how much one can bear to know, and how what we think we know can be distinguished from its opposite, which looks the same. Descartes pointed out that we believe dreams to be true until we wake up, and as Wittgenstein commented, the sun circling the earth would look the same as the earth circling the sun. Othello puts complete faith in the handkerchief as proof of Desdemona's infidelity. He says 'I'll see before I doubt', thinking this rational decision to test a hypothesis and to require 'ocular proof' will protect him from deception and reveal the truth. However, his dependence on the evidence of his eyes (for example, he took Desdemona's tears as proof that she pitied him) deprives him of his analytical faculties.

Iago is the arch-illusionist and has a magician's sleight of hand which deceives the eye. But Othello and Venice are also not what they seem, with an unpleasantness below the surface not acknowledged or known to be there. Like Iago, but for different reasons, Othello comes to consider 'mere suspicion' to be adequate evidence and becomes dependent for his supposed knowledge on his own senses and the deluding demon of Iago. Several characters have shock awakenings when the scales fall from their eyes and they see a loved one in a new and opposite light. Iago destabilises Othello's trust and faith by exposing them as irrational substitutes for knowledge and no match for apparent counter-evidence of a visible and tangible kind.

Limited vision

Honigmann entertains the possibility that Othello may be short-sighted. In Act I scene 2 Iago twice tells Othello who is approaching (although in line 34 Othello recognises Cassio and the Duke's servants), but this may be Iago's way of getting in first with knowledge and making himself indispensable, rather than Shakespeare wanting to suggest that an active military commander is vision-impaired through age. It prepares us, however, for the difficulty of establishing true identities in the play, especially in the dark, and for the realisation that Othello cannot see clearly in a metaphorical sense (this concept is used again in *King Lear*). When Othello asks Iago 'Was not that Cassio parted from my wife?' (III.3.37) it does not mean he is not sure who it was, but that he is surprised, and this question also serves as a device to allow Iago to seize his opportunity to sow the seed of suspicion. Othello becomes dependent on Iago to be his literal and metaphorical eyes and report sights to him, complete with an interpretation. As a result, Othello comes to see the world in the limited and negative way Iago sees it.

However, it could be claimed that, metaphorically, all the characters except Iago have impaired vision. Othello misjudges Iago, Cassio, Desdemona and Emilia. Desdemona miscalculates her father's reaction and loses him, as well as being unable to tell what is bothering Othello and attributing it to pressures of work, wrongly believing him incapable of jealousy; she does not suspect that her maid is untrustworthy and a liar, and does not realise that Iago is the last person she should turn to for help. Cassio is fooled by Iago's fake solicitousness and disastrous advice and appears to understand nothing of Bianca's state of mind (unlike Iago). Emilia appears to be ignorant of her husband's malicious character and of any virtue in Othello. Brabantio 'misperceives' his daughter and his house guest, despite a warning dream. Roderigo goes on believing that Iago is working on his behalf and denies the obvious. That they persist in their misjudgements of each other suggests that people prefer to believe what they want to believe rather than common sense.

Iago could be expected to be vengeful, having lost a much-wanted job, but strangely no one seems to entertain this possibility. Everyone is described as a 'fool' by Iago for not being able to interpret data correctly, and for being deceived by appearances. Innocence and naïvety manifest themselves in the same way as foolishness, however, so it is difficult to argue any difference between Roderigo and Othello, both being Iago's enslaved asses led by the nose. But if the protection against foolishness is cynicism, as Iago thinks it is, is folly preferable?

Overactive imagination

Othello has a strong imagination, that is an ability to see things in his mind, and this trait is significant to his character and to the events of the play, since he sees things which aren't there or misinterprets those which are. We know from his story-telling that he uses graphic description and visual detail. The success of the 'temptation scene' lies not only in Iago's persuasive verbal skills but in his ability to stimulate Othello's imagination so that Othello continues to torment himself even when Iago is absent. Once Othello has a picture of Desdemona's adultery with Cassio in his mind he cannot remove it from his memory and is haunted by it, whereas before: 'I saw't not, thought it not, it harmed not me' (III.3.336). In the narrative of Cassio's sleep-talking and the eavesdropping scene, Iago exploits Othello's need for visual stimulus to keep his suspicions alive. After the wedding night and loss of Desdemona's virginity, Othello, with Iago's help, now sees a fallen woman with an uncontrollable sexual appetite. The cause for which he kills her is his own excessive imagination, which has gone so far as to enable him to see Desdemona and Emilia running a brothel. At the end, he looks to see if the devilish Iago has cloven hooves, so attuned is he to visual imagery. He dies whilst reliving a flashback sequence from his memory.

Superstition is a kind of collective imagination, and there are many examples of irrational beliefs, aphorisms, potions, proverbs and so on in the play: Brabantio's belief in witchcraft; the handkerchief magic; Desdemona's moist palm; itchy eyes which bode weeping; the devil being unkillable. Superstition seems to spread from Brabantio to Othello to Desdemona like a curse or sickness; like jealousy, it cannot be cured because it has no logical basis. The play suggests that beneath the veneer of civilisation lurk primitive ways of responding to life which can be triggered when the characters are under pressure or things appear to be going wrong. People in all periods and cultures revert to a childish state and look for, and find, signs and omens when they need confirmation, guidance, reassurance or an explanation for the inexplicable.

The need to know

The Tree of Knowledge in the garden of Eden tempted Adam and Eve, with Satan's help, to lose their innocence and bliss by eating the forbidden fruit. Likewise Othello succumbs to the desire to know, finds doubt intolerable, and is therefore unable to resist the apple of knowledge the serpent Iago holds out to him. Othello cannot bear it that Iago 'Sees and knows more, much more than he unfolds' (III.3.241) as this makes Iago superior. Curiosity is a basic human drive and Iago destroys Othello by asking the simple question 'How do you know your wife is honest?' and implying that he knows differently.

Thinking and knowing, both ubiquitous verbs in the play, are not the same, though Othello starts out believing that they are because of his trust in rationality. Iago's final torture of Othello is to refuse to give him the knowledge of why he did what he did; his final utterance is, ironically and teasingly, 'what you know, you know'. One cannot both know and remain innocent, because knowledge involves acknowledging evil, hence the expression 'ignorance is bliss'. Othello would not have minded the whole camp enjoying Desdemona carnally, 'So I had nothing known' (III.3.344). Excessive knowledge corrupts, but a little knowledge is a dangerous thing, making one desperate for more and vulnerable to manipulation by the 'knower', who can turn a 'tranquil mind' into that of a 'credulous fool'.

Know thyself

The Delphic oracle exhorted the Ancient Greeks to 'know thyself', and this is a recurrent issue in classical tragedy as well as in Shakespeare's plays. A failure of self-knowledge extends to being unable to know anyone else, to judge oneself or others, or to question one's beliefs, which means a lack of the moral understanding which distinguishes humans from animals. Othello uses the verb 'know' three times in his first speech; 'know' in its various grammatical forms is used 96 times in the play. The paradox of not knowing yourself is that you do not know that you do not know, and can therefore do nothing to avoid becoming a prey to others and to circumstance; had he been aware of his propensity for sudden jealousy, Othello might have been less overcome by it. He seems ignorant of the fact that appearances can be ambiguous and deceptive, and neither forewarned nor forearmed of the way Moors were viewed in Venetian society of the period. Othello cannot see himself except as the reflection in Desdemona's eyes, as a romantic hero, without flaws or weaknesses, or a black visage.

W. H. Auden claimed that Iago is motivated by the desire to know and show what Othello is really like behind the mask of the celebrated warrior and joyful lover. By exposing the weak human hiding behind the façade of reputation he can both avenge himself on Othello and prove the hypocrisy of humanity, thus vindicating his sordid vision and justifying his own attitudes and behaviour as being honest by comparison. The amoral Iago knows that he has to demonstrate that noble abstract virtues don't exist, ethics are an affectation, and love is merely 'a lust of the blood' in order to maintain his own self-esteem. Since these are things he cannot, for various reasons, have himself, he is driven (like Satan) to destroy the paradise from which he is excluded. The question is whether the Othello he reveals is the true Othello or a monster created by Iago which did not previously exist.

Iago knows

Othello tries to justify himself after the murder by saying 'Iago knows'. He thinks he means that Iago knows his wife and Cassio have committed adultery, but of course Iago knows that they haven't, which draws attention to the problems of the meaning and usage of the verb 'to know'. In a wider sense he is implying that Iago is the 'knower' in the play, the repository of facts and wisdom, the counsellor and watcher who has power and authority because of his knowledge. Iago knows more than the other characters know themselves — how others feel about them, their future and present situations — and can predict their responses with what seems to be a supernatural prescience. He knows things he cannot explicably know, such as the details of the elopement, Othello's imminent posting to Cyprus, Bianca's feelings for Cassio — but which he has somehow divined by being alert and observant the whole time, by accurate character assessment, and by his understanding of human nature.

What does Emilia know?

There is disagreement about just how much Emilia knows. For example, in Act V scene 2 real surprise would look the same as fake surprise, so we cannot be sure whether she knew of Iago's plans for the handkerchief. In Cinthio's version of the story she does know, and Honigmann is inclined to think Shakespeare's Emilia also knows — she calls her husband 'wayward' (III.3.289) — but is too frightened to speak out; Iago has ordered her to plead ignorance about the theft: 'Be not acknown on't' (III.3.316). That she is, however, deceived in her estimation of her husband is suggested by her appearing to believe that Iago is sorry about Cassio's dismissal, and it is unlikely she would curse her husband, even in pretence (Act IV scene 2), since curses were taken very seriously and could not be undone. That she calls her husband nothing worse than 'wayward', meaning capricious, suggests she does not fully comprehend his capacity for evil. There are extra ironies and poignancy to be achieved by her having unwittingly destroyed her mistress by not asking questions of her husband, who is in any case unlikely to have confided in her from what we know of their relationship and his view of women. In Act V scene 2 she repeats the phrase 'My husband!' so often that it is difficult to believe she is not genuinely incredulous. Her sudden speaking out and decision to risk death in defiance of Iago suggests she has just gained shocking new knowledge about the man she is married to and would rather 'ne'er go home' (V.2.196) than go home to him.

Point of view

Events look very different depending upon one's point of view, and this creates tension for the audience. We see a very different Iago from the one everyone else sees, and this makes us feel complicit and helpless. We see Iago on stage watching others nearly all the time, which forces us to see things as he sees them and realise how incriminating they look — such as the hand-kissing between Cassio and Desdemona. We can see Othello as Iago sees him, which again is damaging. There are also strong visual images for the audience to assimilate: Othello's blackness and how he stands out from the other characters, especially the fair Desdemona; Desdemona's angelic and childlike appearance getting ready for bed and the pathos of her vulnerability in her white nightgown; Othello writhing on the floor in a fit; Othello striking Desdemona; the suffocation. Because we do not see their relationship before the problems begin, we feel unsure about the validity of their love and the security of its foundation, as it is presented as a past narrative by Othello, with a conflicting version by Brabantio. Many of the main themes of the play are transferred to the experience of the audience, and doubting the evidence of one's eyes is one of them.

We see a lot of Iago (Othello is absent for half of the play) and he has plenty of opportunity to seduce the audience. He foists his monstrous vision on us as the rational one by showing that the world-view of others is based on things demonstrably untrue (e.g. that Venice is a virtuous city). He shows us that under a sophisticated surface lies primitive instinct; that nature is unnatural; that fortune favours evil; that nobility means foolishness; and that white is black. He says 'This is how it is', and then proves it to be so. We see human degradation with our own eyes in watching Othello's decline, and it confirms reality as we know it, in which there are no divine and pure heroines, or brave heroes motivated by a noble cause, or any other paragons who belong to the world of fiction. On the other hand, one could argue that Iago is an illusionist who imposes on Othello and the audience a vision so realistic that we are left wondering which is the reality and which the fantasy.

Themes

As with other aspects of the play, binary oppositions are reflected within the themes, and one could say that opposition is in itself a main theme. Many of the themes are also built into the structure of the play, so that, for instance, division is represented in plot terms by the sea journey and change of location. The main themes of jealousy, honesty, seeing and knowing have already been discussed.

Division — a word used several times in the play (e.g. IV.1.229) to refer to the breaking of family, marital and friendship bonds caused by fate, culture, circumstance or malice. Desdemona perceives a 'divided duty' between her father and husband; the sea divides Venice and Cyprus; Othello and Desdemona are on different ships. Othello progressively becomes divided from his father-in-law, his best friend, his wife, his employers and himself. The ships break up in the storm, unable to 'hold the mortise', a symbol for Othello's impending breakdown. Suicide is an act of division, the self destroying the self against all natural instincts of self-preservation, and particularly so in Othello's case where one Othello is the Christian killer and the other the Moslem killed. His character is divided between the imaginative romantic and the rational man of action. He is unable to tolerate ambiguity, to reconcile a divided mind, and he speaks of himself in both the first and the third person.

Isolation — Othello is isolated from the beginning of the play, when the Venetians talk disparagingly and threateningly of him to each other but he is absent. He is on stage much less than Iago and is late to arrive in Act I and Act II and many of the individual scenes. Othello is often seen on stage standing apart from others who are talking to each other, or whom he has to address as an audience. This isolation distorts his view, and is exploited further by Iago, who fills the vacuum left by the go-between Cassio and makes Othello dependent upon him for information about the others. It seems beyond Othello's capabilities to communicate intelligibly with Desdemona, and his attempt to talk to Emilia is equally thwarted by misunderstanding. His dialogues with her, Desdemona and Iago are more like dramatic monologues than conversations. Other characters find communication difficult, even those in supposedly close relationships. In many ways Othello is like the island of Cyprus, remote from civilisation and vulnerable to attack. Desdemona's lack of family and friends on her first foray from the safety of her house (she is deprived of the company of father and husband the same evening) adds to the pathos of her situation.

Perdition — (from Latin *perdere*: to lose) means to lose one's soul, something Othello is anxious to avoid as a Christian, for himself and Desdemona. Perdition and its opposite, salvation, are mentioned many times in the play by Othello, Cassio while drunk, and Iago. The wider sense of loss includes that of the handkerchief, symbolic of loss of innocence, reputation and love. Desdemona loses her father, and he her; Othello and Cassio lose their honour; Iago loses a position and his humanity; Roderigo loses Desdemona, his money and his life.

Telling tales — relevant in both senses, betraying a secret to get someone into trouble and making up fictional stories. Iago tells tales about Desdemona and Cassio to Othello, Desdemona and Othello to Roderigo, Desdemona and Othello to Brabantio, Bianca to Cassio, Cassio to Othello, Cassio to Montano, Othello to Lodovico, and Emilia (and women generally) to Desdemona. Iago accuses Bianca with 'tell's another tale' (V.1.125). Ironically it is Othello who introduces tale-telling by weaving a web of words to make Desdemona fall in love with his life-story, and Brabantio tells tales to the Duke about the witchcraft practised on his daughter by the guest who earned invitations to his home because of his tale-telling ability. Othello has been accused of 'narrative self-fashioning' (quoted in the *Arden* introduction) and editing of the past, with his inconsistent fabrication of the origin of the handkerchief, and his exaggeration of military exploits and things seen on his travels. He ends the play by demanding that Lodovico tell the Senate his story, and he dies telling the tale of his victory over the Turkish traitor at Aleppo. He himself becomes a new traveller's tale to be told in Venice on the return of Lodovico and Gratiano, just as Desdemona, who tells Barbary's tale and that of the Willow Song, is turned into one of the romantic legends she is so fond of. Story-tellers have a traditional and powerful role in literature (e.g. Odysseus, Scheherazade, the Ancient Mariner), and the spinner of stories is able to spellbind with suspense unwary captive listeners. Tales are dangerous because fictions cannot be trusted, lead one astray or can be used to deceive; they are the appearance of truth but really the stuff of dreams, fantasy and faulty memory.

Deception — 'Honest Iago' is not the only deceiver in the play. Othello has deceived Brabantio, with ulterior motives for his frequent house visits and use of Cassio as go-between. Is he deceiving himself, the Senate or both when he assures the Duke that he isn't interested in sex and this isn't why he wants Desdemona with him in Cyprus? Cassio takes a mistress in Cyprus but does not want Othello to see him 'womaned' (III.4.191). He begins the play with a pretence to Iago that he knows nothing about any relationship or secret marriage between Othello and Desdemona, though it turns out later that he 'went between them very oft' (III.3.99). He is 'framed to make women false', a causer of deception in others. Desdemona is condemned by her father as deceitful. She does, understandably but fatally, lie to Othello about the whereabouts of the handkerchief, giving Othello his only real proof of her dishonesty, and dies with a lie on her lips, claiming that black is white, i.e. the Moor is innocent. We remember that she pretended to be frightened of Othello when she was really attracted to him. Emilia is obviously a deceiver. Venice is a deceptive city, apparently without robbery according to Brabantio's complacent claim ('This is Venice/My house is not a grange' I.1.105–06) and the pinnacle of civilisation, but actually full of 'super-subtle' characters. Perhaps the play is suggesting that there is a moral difference between Iago's black lies for personal advantage and the white lies of those who have no choice or are committed to a higher cause. Alternatively, it may be making the point that in a world which has become darkened by sinfulness and corruption (Venice, Iago or just a fallen world generally) and where honesty has been hijacked by the dishonest, it is impossible for even 'good' characters to maintain truthfulness and a correspondence between appearance and reality.

Betrayal — everyone betrays someone, deliberately or unwittingly, or is believed to have done so; the word is used in the play, along with 'traduced', and the idea of the Turks as traitors. It would seem that love and betrayal are two sides of the same coin, whether it is love between parent and child, friends, colleagues or lovers. The Willow Song reminds us that stories of romance and war, mythology and literature, have always been based on the idea of a promise not kept, or a defection to the enemy side. This makes faith and trust seem doomed and foolish, and oaths and pledges meaningless.

Excess — excess of any kind (it is a main theme in *Romeo and Juliet* too) in medieval and Elizabethan times was seen as a loss of control and a step on the road to damnation. There are numerous examples in the play of extremes of behaviour and utterance: Othello saying farewell to war and himself because he suspects his wife of infidelity; his bombastic way of speaking and exaggerated tales of 'men whose heads/Do grow beneath their shoulders'; the reunion on Cyprus being 'too much of joy'; his falling into a fit; Cassio's excessive drinking and his disproportionate condemnation of the demon drink afterwards; Othello's punishment of Cassio with 'nevermore be officer of mine' (II.3.243); his killing a wife for alleged adultery (an excessive response even if she were guilty). Excess is the hallmark of romance, and Othello has lost touch with reality and lives like a fictional character, as does Desdemona with her total subservience to an ideal and to her lord and an acceptance of death which is hard to distinguish from suicide. She gets carried away in her bantering with Iago and in her pleading for Cassio; as the *Arden* introduction puts it, 'she does not know when to stop'. Othello admits he has lost his temper (literally meaning he has lost his moderation) in Act II scene 3, and Cassio is described as being 'rash and very sudden in choler', sharing Othello's vice of wrath, i.e. extreme anger. When Desdemona tells us that Othello 'will return incontinent' (IV.3.11) the secondary meaning of 'unable to contain himself' is as relevant as the primary one, 'immediately'. It is Cassio's 'excess of laughter' (IV.1.99) which puts the signature on Desdemona's death warrant. Othello's speech (III.3.450–59) uses 'never' four times in six lines, making it an immoderate oath, and he finally admits to the excesses of being 'Perplexed in the extreme' (V.2.342) and of loving 'not wisely, but too well' (V.2.340). Iago, on the other hand, has what the *Arden* introduction calls an 'inhuman self-command' and we never see him overcome by emotion.

Chaos — meant more than just disorder; it was an image of a return to a state prior to the creation of the universe, i.e. the black void. For chaos to come again the world must be de-created through a 'gross revolt' against nature — this is what Desdemona is accused of in her choice of husband by Iago, and in her lustfulness by Othello. The foundations and bonds of society dissolve if marriage, trust, justice, reputation and knowledge are proved to be illusions, and if humanity can be undone by devilish, bestial and inhumane behaviour. Othello's beautiful world is deconstructed by Iago, leaving nothing intact; Desdemona's 'goodness' ceases to be a virtue and undoes 'her credit with the Moor' (II.3.349). The barrier against chaos is reason; Othello asks Iago for a reason, and is refused, the last time he speaks to him. Without a cause the universe makes no sense and madness and chaos rule (an idea explored further in *King Lear*).

Service — is a concept integral to Christianity and feudalism, as well as to the social and family structures of the period. The army in particular is based on rank and there is much harping on the titles of captain, general and the disputed lieutenancy. Women must serve their fathers and husbands; Emilia is Desdemona's servant; Othello is a servant of Venice and dies claiming to have 'done the state some service'. Iago the ensign is meant to serve Othello, but becomes his master; he uses 'lord' sarcastically and dedicates himself to 'wrong'd Othello's service' (III.3.464). The master/servant relationship was considered crucial to an understanding of humanity and its roles and was the expression of the civilising virtues of nobility, trust, loyalty, honour, love and harmony.

Images

Shakespeare's imagery repays close study, as each play has its own peculiar and recurring group of images in addition to the typical and traditional images of the Elizabethan period, such as those pertaining to heaven and hell, fire and water, bonds and divisions. The language of the tragedies is dominated by life-threatening images of evil, poison, disease and violence, echoing Biblical imagery. In Shakespeare plays, images are often literalised metaphors, e.g. Othello's blackness is both his actual skin colour and a representation of evil; the conceptual adulterous bed becomes the real marital bed in the final act. In addition to reinforcing themes, imagery gives atmosphere and progression to a text, helps to delineate character, and provides integrity, pattern and meaning. The images in *Othello*, like so much else, tend to work in pairs of opposites, e.g. dark and light, which can then be seen to reverse themselves or become indistinguishable from each other.

Animals — Iago has what Heilman has called a 'barnyard view of life'. His animals are loathsome and he favours those associated at the time with sex, ugliness and the devil: toads, goats and monkeys. In addition to these, and flies and spiders, he refers to: Barbary horse, ass, old black ram, beast with two backs, guinea-hen, baboon, cats and blind puppies. Several of them are used in the context of the act of copulation. Othello starts to adopt this low imagery — which Iago uses throughout the play — from the end of Act III; this is a sign of how much he has been degraded verbally and mentally, and his behaviour soon falls to a level which corresponds with his ignoble diction.

Words — Iago's last word in the play is 'word'; when he has twisted all words out of recognition, he renounces them and will never speak again. There are numerous references to tongues, mouths, speech and silence. Othello is subdued, though a sword could not have done so, by the power of words made manifest in Iago, who, like Satan, can cause the fall of man by seductive speech. Wittgenstein said 'the limits of my language are the limits of my mind. All I know is what I have words for'; both Othello and Iago have limitations of vision and understanding caused by the restrictions of their high and low vocabularies respectively. Words are beginnings and ends, causes and effects: Desdemona, strangely 'free of speech', initiated the romance with Othello by speaking out first; she is still speaking beyond apparent death; Emilia is frequently told to close her mouth by Iago, and his killing of her is to achieve this aim; Cassio is struck dumb at a crucial moment and then spends the rest of the play trying to speak to Othello, who says of him, when he thinks he is dead, 'his mouth is stopped'. Othello and Iago have the control of speech-making in the play, and it is a matter of debate who gets the last word: Iago will be tortured to 'ope [his] lips' (V.2.303).

Turning — Iago is good at turning something into its negative opposite ('So will I turn her virtue into pitch', II.3.350) and the word is much used to reinforce the idea of inconstancy and betrayal. Iago's talent for transformation gives the sinister impression that he is a sorcerer. Another trick of Iago's is to turn himself into something he isn't by assuming at will qualities he does not possess or believe, such as servitude (he uses 'sir' for effect when currying favour); Coleridge believed that Iago shows 'how a wicked man employs his real feelings, as well as assumes those most alien from his own, as instruments of his purpose'. Personal events which should be private (e.g. wedding nights, matters of conjugal fidelity, Brabantio's discovery of his daughter's marriage) are turned into public performances so that other possible reactions are ruled out by considerations of saving face. Othello insults Desdemona in public with 'she can turn, and turn, and yet go on,/And turn again.' (IV.1.255–56). We watch in horror as Othello turns Turk, i.e. turns into an opposite of his former self, and Cyprus has this effect on the 'Italians' generally (II.3.164). Some squire hinting at Emilia's unfaithfulness with Othello 'turned [Iago's] wit the seamy side without' (IV.2.145); Iago claims Roderigo has been turned the wrong side out by love (II.3.48). It is a recurring motif in the play that love and jealousy cause changes to an opposite state.

Poison — Iago uses it to describe his own attack on Othello ('I'll pour this pestilence into his ear', II.3.346; 'The Moor already changes with my poison', III.3.322); his ruining of Brabantio's life ('poison his delight', I.1.69); and to describe the acute pain of jealousy. Iago is poison personified, an agent which destroys healthy tissue and kills its host, something created by nature but which behaves unnaturally and undoes creation and goodness. Like Satan, he is the venomous serpent who will spoil the beauty he cannot have for himself. The image of the three dead bodies on stage at the end 'poisons sight' (V.2.360).

Jewels — Roderigo and Othello make reference to jewels, but very differently: for the former they are a symbol of wealth and a means of attempting to corrupt

Desdemona's virtue; for the latter they are an image of purity, beauty and worth, which he loses when he throws away the heavenly pearls of Desdemona and his own soul. Brabantio also calls Desdemona 'jewel', in his case meaning a valuable possession. Jewels were often the spoils of war, as well as gifts from lovers, and Desdemona could be viewed as the prize claimed by Othello from the city of Venice for his services to the state.

Pregnancy — leads to birth, the end result of sex, with which Iago is much preoccupied in thought and utterance. Othello has been garrisoned in Venice for 'nine moons' and the secret marriage is the product of his relationship with Desdemona. Iago's plan will bring forth a 'monstrous birth' from the dark womb of time 'to the world's light'. Iago sees conception, a word much used in its various forms and double meaning, as the generation and growth of his own ideas and their transference into the gardens/minds of others. The murder of Desdemona is the outcome of the planting of the seed of jealousy in Othello's fertile imagination. None of the characters have children (Brabantio disowns his only child) or living siblings (Othello's brother is dead); compared to the other multi-generational tragedies and late plays there is a noticeable sterility in *Othello*. Brabantio is concerned about potential bestial offspring from the marriage; childless Iago regards his ideas as his progeny, which could be called the spawn of the devil.

Sea — the 'dangerous' chaotic element between Venice and Cyprus, during the crossing of which Othello possibly loses his pole position (he arrives last), his confidence (the elements attack him), and his faith in Desdemona (her father has sown a seed of distrust). It also symbolises, in traditional ballads, inconstancy, separation, turmoil, overwhelming emotion, weeping, hostile fate, death, and loss of a loved one. Othello is the main user of sea imagery, which matches his progress through the play from quiet grandeur to disturbed flux to uncontrollable rage. The sea, like Othello, has two moods, benevolent and malevolent.

Traps — webs and nets are images for Iago the fly-trapping spider, and the tangled complexities caused by deception. Catching prey is a power issue which divides characters into predator and victims. Othello and Desdemona are 'entrapped' on an island and in Iago's web. Other relevant examples of figurative language are: 'enfettered', 'enmeshed', 'ensnare', 'embayed', 'ensheltered' (the last three words are unique in Shakespeare), 'ensteeped', 'enwheel', 'encave' (these three words are coinages by Shakespeare). The prefix 'en' means to surround, to imprison, without hope of extrication.

Gardening — As one critic has put it, 'Iago is strangely preoccupied with plants'. Adam was the first gardener and controller of nature; Iago uses gardening imagery (e.g. I.3.317–22, II.3.365–66, III.3.420) as if he were an infernal travesty of the keeper of Eden. Iago's homely wisdom on horticulture — 'fruits that blossom first will first be ripe' — is obvious yet sinister, as though he is in charge of the creation cycle of planting, nurturing and harvesting, and as if what he is growing is a natural and inevitable product of human nature. Seeds and conception, pregnancy and birth are all images associated with Iago the un-creator. Those prevented from advancement by an accident of birth (like Edmund in *King Lear*) have nothing to lose by adopting a 'survival of the fittest' ideology and emulating nature's ruthlessness towards the weak. Iago plants seeds in fertile soil which grow extremely large and bear monstrous fruit, watered by chance, fate and time.

Hell — there are 64 diabolic images or references in the play, though none at all in the source story. The hell imagery originates with Iago and is taken up by Othello like an infection in Act III, with an increasing number of images in each act as the poison spreads: 10, 11, 13, 14, 16 respectively. Othello sees Iago as a creature from hell at the end, as realisation finally dawns; his progress through the play could be compared to a descent into hell. Iago uses a mixture of holy and hellish vocabulary — 'holy writ', 'baptism', 'virtue', 'sulphur' — as if both heaven and hell are equal fictions to him, or as if he can so easily, like a magician, turn one into the other; sacred into profane. Othello, who uses Christian and Biblical language throughout the play, calls upon Heaven to sanction the hellish murder of the divine Desdemona.

Blood — paradoxically the means of life and the image of death; it also means passion, particularly anger and revenge, and is the antithesis to the 'safer guides' of judgement. Othello gives himself over to being ruled by 'blood' when he loses his temper over Cassio's street fighting; he then uses the image repeatedly until the end of the play, most strikingly in the line 'blood, blood, blood' (III.3.448). It has other relevant meanings to do with natural instinct (as opposed to the intellect), sensuality, and the heat of sexual activity. Loss of virginity is signified by blood; the handkerchief is spotted with red.

Eyes — 'sight', 'visage', 'gaze', 'ocular' are used in the play, in addition to 'eyes' and repeated use of all forms of the verb 'to see'. Cinthio refers to 'the Moor, who had loved the lady more than his very eyes'; Othello refers to Desdemona as 'this heavenly sight'. The precious and vulnerable organs of seeing enable us to interpret and judge people, places and actions, and are the means of falling in love. Brabantio thinks Desdemona must have been given a potion to affect her eyesight if she could want a 'sooty bosom' as a husband. One can have eyes but a 'false gaze' and be blind to faults or to the truth, and if eyes can be blindfolded, as Othello's are in many instances, they are an instrument to plague us rather than an organ of relevation.

Black and white — the two main events are a marriage and a murder, the white and black 'book-ends' to the play which create a shocking contrast. Black and white images, moral and visual, dominate the play and are used by all the characters as semantic clusters signifying good or evil, but one can't be sure which is which as they change into each other, as Desdemona's (white) virtue is turned into (black) pitch (II.3.350). Good qualities suddenly turn into their opposite at the toss of a coin in a way which casts doubt on their original value, e.g. love to hate, trust to doubt, possession to loss, honour to dishonour. Shakespeare seems to suggest that there is another face or side to everything, which fate or circumstance can bring to the surface, and that therefore nothing is certain or absolute and everything is a question of perception. Black is stronger than white, as clean over time becomes dirty, innocence is replaced by experience, and the candle is extinguished. In nature, the diseased plant cannot make itself healthy again, only spread its corruption to others. Black always wins the game, because white does not even realise a game is being played.

The handkerchief

Thomas Rymer, in his *A Short View of Tragedy*, 1693, summed up *Othello* as: 'so much ado, so much stress...about an handkerchief' and asked 'Why was not this called the tragedy of the handkerchief?' Although this criticism was refuted by George Gordon in 1944 in his essay 'Othello, or the Tragedy of the Handkerchief', it is true that many critics have focused on the 'napkin' and dismissed the play as being no more than a domestic drama because of it. The handkerchief is, however, more than just a square of cloth; it means different things to different people and is an indicator of character, a test of relationships, the key to the plot and a symbol of major themes in the play.

A handkerchief in those days was often an heirloom or part of a dowry, hand-made from expensive fabric, usually silk, and personally embroidered. Only the nobility possessed such a luxury item. Larger than today's handkerchiefs, it would not be used for blowing the nose but as a decorative accessory. Its role in medieval literature was as a romantic love token either given to a suitor or dropped to provoke a chivalrous response.

Desdemona's handkerchief was, according to Othello's romantic account, woven by a 200-year-old sibyl (a female prophet), using silk from sacred worms and dye from the hearts of mummified virgins. However, he then tells two versions of its story: that his father gave it to his mother and warned her that if she lost it his love for her would die; that an Egyptian gave it to his mother and told her it would subdue his father, and that she gave it to Othello on her death to pass on to his future wife. Obviously, both versions are relevant to the play, but raise questions about truth, faith, superstition, and the power of matter over mind to lead to self-fulfilling prophecy. Othello is lying to Desdemona, consciously or unconsciously, as both versions cannot be true; he is also expressing his primitive beliefs for the first time. Being spotted with strawberries, the handkerchief could represent blood droplets on white sheets, a depiction of deflowering or the 'fruits of love' Othello is looking forward to on the wedding night, but which afterwards he may retain in his mind as an image of Desdemona's impurity.

The handkerchief functions as a test of knowledge of each others' characters for all the main characters in the play: Bianca guesses wrongly about how Cassio came by it; Cassio wrongly assumes that Bianca won't mind copying it for him; Desdemona does not suspect where it is or why; Othello wrongly believes that Desdemona gave it to Cassio; Cassio fails to recognise it as Desdemona's, though apparently she always had it about her person; Emilia appears not to know why Iago wants it. Only Iago knows so well how the minds of all the others work that he can predict the progression of the handkerchief.

Different views

For Othello, the handkerchief is a romantic object he gave to Desdemona and asked her to cherish; therefore to him it is a symbol of his love for her and of the faith and trust which bind their marriage — by losing it she is rejecting him. He sees it as a symbol of Desdemona's body, which he thinks she has given to someone else; it is the privacy of Desdemona made public. Since she is herself a valuable emblem of Othello's success, the handkerchief is therefore the emblem of that emblem. It is also a sentimental link with his mother, a symbol of his parents' marriage, an 'antique token' linking him to his childhood past, a superstitious talisman, a magic which must be respected or something precious will be destroyed. He associates it with beauty, intimacy, physical contact, tenderness, the female duty to sooth the male troubled brow, and these can be stolen from him and enjoyed by others, it seems. The loss of the handkerchief ('perdition') equals not only the loss of love but the loss of Desdemona's soul, as he sees it. It is conclusive evidence of his wife's adultery. On the other hand, by rejecting it as 'too little' he rejects Desdemona's attempt to minister to him, and therefore her love. He causes it to fall to the floor and lie unnoticed, so that ironically he is the one who separates her from it and causes the chain of tragic events stemming from its loss.

For Desdemona, it is a love gift, a lucky charm to make Othello love her as his father loved his mother, and her only link with his family and his past. She kisses it and talks to it, as a substitute for the physical presence of Othello. It suggests her immaturity that she treats is as a child treats a comfort cloth, unable to be parted from it. Her offer to use it as a bandage to bind his head shows her sympathy and wifely duty. Her reaction to being reminded by Othello of the provenance of the handkerchief (Act III scene 4) is uncharacteristically brief and enigmatic ('Is't possible?' 'Indeed!' 'Is't true?'). These utterances could mean many things: she is desperately stalling for time and trying to remember where it might have gone; she is fascinated by what he is saying; this is the first time she has heard the story; she is puzzled because this is not what she has previously been told about it; she is dismissive and sceptical about the magic power it is supposed to have. They seem to have reverted to the roles of their courtship, whereby he tells her a fantastic tale and she plays the attentive listener and makes appropriately amazed and appreciative noises, except that now the story has become sinister reality.

For Iago, the handkerchief in itself is a silly toy, but it is useful as the provider of the 'ocular proof' of Desdemona's infidelity which Othello has demanded. It reassures him that fate is on his side, since it so conveniently materialises just when he needs it. (There is a question about why he has 'wooed' Emilia to steal it 'a hundred times' if the plot against Othello is a new idea.) It reassures him how clever an opportunist he is to think up a use for it so quickly, and it enables him to go beyond proof of guilt and proceed to the next stages of sentencing and execution.

Shakespeare makes Emilia pick up the dropped handkerchief, rather than have Iago find it — or steal it as in Cinthio — which adds many extra dimensions to the play's relationships and coincidences. Because Emilia also hates Othello and her mistress's 'most filthy bargain', it is plausible for her to take the handkerchief to spite the original owner of it as an unconscious undoing of the marriage. Her part in the theft draws attention to her problematic relationship with Iago and need to please her husband (a social reality despite her views on marriage); it makes Desdemona seem isolated and beset on all sides by enemies. Furthermore, it creates irony and adds to the theme of betrayal by someone trusted; it adds emotional complexity and suggests that Emilia's feeling of guilt may explain her reason for later risking death to clear Desdemona's name; it gives neatness to the plot, as all six main characters (three couples) plus Othello's parents have the handkerchief pass through their hands and are affected by it in some way. It links those who have never met, and can be seen as a symbol of malevolent change, turning loving relationships into destructive ones.

The audience feels that the evidence against Desdemona is very flimsy until she cannot produce the handkerchief, and then we realise that this little thing has become a hostile character in the play and is going to be the nail in her coffin. We are struck by the irony, tragedy and irrationality of being condemned to death for dropping your handkerchief. It seems to the audience as well as the characters to be an instrument of fate, either what they most want to find or can least afford to lose. For the audience too it seems there must be some 'magic in the web of it', for it to be the 'cause' of so much havoc; it also correlates with the other web of Iago's machinations and seems to be in the service of his malevolent will. There is **poetic justice** in it finally becoming tangible proof of Iago's guilt.

Doubles: language and meaning

Verse and prose

Verse is language which is rhythmically organised according to particular patterns of metre and the arrangement of lines. Prose is discourse which is not constructed according to any measurable pattern and is not set out in lines, but which can still have a rhythm. In plays of Shakespeare's time and earlier, verse was the conventional medium of all literary discourse, including drama, and his plays all consist largely of **blank (unrhymed) verse**.

Verse tended to be given to noble and royal characters, expressing romantic or elevated feelings, and at certain heightened moments they use **rhyming couplets**. These are also used at the ends of scenes to give them an air of finality — often sinister — or for spells, songs or some other special form of discourse. Couplets also suggest common wisdom is being quoted, as in Act I scene 3 when Brabantio and the Duke exchange sententious advice. Prose was generally reserved for characters of lower social status, for comic or domestic scenes, or to indicate secrecy or conspiracy (Iago and drunken Cassio communicate in prose, and Iago and Roderigo when plotting in Act II scene 1).

The monotony of several hours of blank verse is avoided by metrical irregularities, incomplete and shared lines, **enjambement**, **caesuras** and stress reversals; these all obscure the normal verse rhythm and give variety, so that the audience is not usually conscious of the play's dialogue being mainly in verse. Close analysis of the verse reveals that these techniques, as well as having a dramatic effect, can indicate the characters' attitudes and feelings. It is always significant and needs to be interpreted if a character who normally uses verse switches to prose and vice versa. Characters who suddenly become less fluent, articulate or capable of speaking in a smooth rhythm are often undergoing emotional disturbance or rapid thinking. This is particularly noticeable in Othello's speeches in Acts III and IV, and in Iago's incomplete line (V.2.178). You should be aware of the prose sequences in the play and the effect created by their contrast with what precedes and follows in each case. You also need to note which characters rarely use or are uncomfortable with prose, such as Desdemona, and which change according to their interlocutor or context, like Emilia. Iago moves easily between verse and prose, as one would expect.

There are different types of prose, in terms of register and complexity of syntax, and this plays a role in the delineation of character. A formal register used in an intimate situation, such as Othello to the sleeping Desdemona at the beginning of Act V scene 2, is often an indication that a character wishes to distance her/himself from what she/he is doing and justify it. Colloquial diction in an official setting is equally odd and in need of comment, as in Act IV scene 1 when Othello talks inappropriately to Lodovico. Simple monosyllables, when repeated, convey intense and inarticulate feeling, such as Othello's 'O, blood, blood, blood!' (III.3.448). When he uses the affectionate words 'wretch', 'wench' and 'my girl' of Desdemona the audience's attention is drawn to the chilling incongruity between language and action, highlighting his mental struggle.

'You' is either a plural or an indication of respect to someone of higher authority, whereas 'thou', singular, suggests familiarity or affection, or talking down to a social inferior. This meant that it could be used as an insult or to suggest an irregular intimacy, and, conversely, using 'you' to a family member would convey coldness. In *Othello* the respectful use of 'you' has been replaced by 'thee' between all the characters by the final act, as evidence of the breakdown of relationships, hierarchy and normality.

Double talk

Iago has the ability to use language and events to kill two birds with one stone. He significantly refers to Janus, the two-faced god, and is himself committed to 'double knavery' (I.3.388). He is a white man who speaks with forked tongue, and where he is concerned the medium (double-talking) is the message (double-crossing). In Act II scene 3 he both condemns and excuses Cassio's fault, and in Act III scene 3 he wins Othello's trust by offering support and sympathy, but he is actually insulting and belittling him. He simultaneously slanders Cassio and criticises Othello's lack of judgement to Montano in Act II scene 3 — whilst still giving the impression of being honest and a loyal friend to both. Setting up Roderigo to attack Cassio could deliver double benefit to Iago if they kill each other. Getting Othello to kill Desdemona and then himself scores double points.

In a play dealing with duplicity, seeming and opposites, one would expect the language of *Othello* to contain elements of doubleness; the word 'double' is itself used several times, e.g. 'double-damned' (IV.2.36). Othello is sometimes called the general and sometimes called the Moor, which draws attention to contrasting aspects of his character and the two contradictory attitudes of others towards him. As well as two Othellos, there are two Iagos, the 'honest Iago', and the behind-the-scenes dishonest one. As the *Penguin* introduction points out, 'while Othello's characteristic image is the metaphor, Iago's is the simile' (p. 43), i.e. the stated double. His conscious use of parallelisms and symmetry, typical of the unfeeling cynic, has been described as the 'intellectual, hyper-conscious child of the brain, combining skilful ingenuity with calculation' (Clemen). Iago likes alliteration and puns, dabbles in doubling: 'parley to provocation', 'potations pottle-deep', 'potent in potting' all occur in one scene (Act II scene 3).

Oxymoronic phrases show that paradox is built into the language of the play: 'Divinity of hell!' (II.3.340); 'excellent wretch' (III.3.90); 'fair devil' (III.3.475);

'this sorrow's heavenly' (V.2.21); 'an honourable murderer' (V.2.291); 'honest Iago'. There are also several words in frequent use in the play which are ambiguous: lying (physically and verbally), committed (action and adultery), satisfied (logically and sexually), solicit (request and sexually importune), conceive (mentally and physically), credit (worth and belief), faithful (having faith and being chaste), incontinent (immediate and unable to restrain sexual appetite). Iago is deliberate in his use of sexual innuendo and **double entendre**, as with 'soliciting' at the end of Act II, but presumably Desdemona and Cassio are not; Cassio asks that Emilia will 'procure' him some 'access' to Desdemona (III.1.35).

These ambiguities achieve various purposes: stressing the naïvety of Desdemona and Cassio, contributing to the overall impression that everything is double-sided, raising the issue of how one decides between two conflicting interpretations, showing how Iago's language spreads and dominates as the play progresses, and keeping a sexual undercurrent running throughout a play the *Arden* introduction describes as 'sex-drenched'. Emilia's 'Never, my lord' (IV.2.9) could equally be the truth or a lie. Underlying the attitudes to Othello in the play is the unrelated but symptomatic pair of words 'barbary' and 'barbarian'.

Another group of words seems to dominate the play because of constant reiteration: there are 52 'honests', 29 'lieutenants', 25 'lies' and 'devils', and over 20 'beds'. Saying something many times gives it credibility, especially to the unsuspecting hearer, or it suggests an obsession. To the suspicious, it is conclusive evidence, and Desdemona's use of Cassio's name has this effect on Othello. Reiteration also contributes to the theme of excess, and parallels the duplication of events which include a double climax, e.g. Iago's suspicion of Emilia's adultery; Desdemona 'hath deceived her father, and may thee'; Cassio being attacked by Roderigo; Desdemona being cast off; ships arriving from Venice; Othello killing the Turk. If something has happened once, it can happen again, logically, and this sets up a self-fulfilling expectation that it will.

Competing styles

There are two distinct speech registers in the play, literary and colloquial, and contradictory perceptions, e.g. war is glorious for Othello, but just a 'trade' for Iago. Othello is associated with idealised, romantic and literary language, which has an effect on his character portrayal. He uses what the *Arden* introduction calls 'elastic abstractions' which 'slide and skid from one sense to another', e.g. heaven, love, nature, soul. He also refers to precious and heavenly objects, such as pearls and chrysolite. In Acts I and II, and again in Act V, Othello's speeches are characterised by theatrical bombast and high rhetoric, full of abstract nouns and clichés of the glory of war. The effect is that, while sounding noble and heroic, he seems to belong to a legendary realm rather than the land of reality. His exotic and polysyllabic diction and complex sentence structures are incongruous with the practicalities of battle and survival. He shares some grand style characteristics and romantic ideals with Cassio, but none at all with Iago, which may explain his choice of lieutenant. Othello and Desdemona seem only able to communicate in the language of religion and romantic fiction.

Iago uses simple, commercial and domestic diction. He calls a spade a spade and is brisk and materialistic in his speech; he talks about money and body parts, and refers to women as housewives or strumpets, making everything concrete and therefore low, turning love into farmyard copulation. His practical diction distinguishes him from higher-born characters and reveals that he is not a gentleman; Cassio's speech is very different from Iago's, as is his attitude to life and women. This is particularly noticeable in Act II scene 3 where Iago describes Desdemona as 'wanton', 'sport for Jove', 'full of game' and 'provocation' in contrast to Cassio's description of her as 'exquisite', 'fresh', 'delicate', 'modest' and 'perfection'. Iago's reference in III.1 to 'clyster-pipes', which were used to give enemas, is typical of his grossly physical and degrading view of the human body. However, because he describes a world the audience can relate to, and even his figurative language is down-to-earth — concerning plants and animals — Iago seems closer to reality and to the audience than Othello and his flights of fancy.

Sometimes Iago uses long Latinate words or tortuous syntax for what the *Arden* introduction calls a 'bamboozling' effect. He can go from false courtesy to brutal directness in one bound, and his switch from 'you' to 'thou' when addressing his superiors is indicative of this. He is a connoisseur of other characters' language and what it reveals, which he comments on. He actualises Othello's metaphors, so whereas Othello refers to 'blood' as an image for passion or, later, revenge, Iago adopts it as the physical acts of stabbing and cutting; whereas Othello sees Desdemona as a jewel, Iago is interested in jewellery. By getting Othello down to his level, the level of a common or garden domestic handkerchief, Iago wins the battle of styles.

Paradoxes and ironies

Paradoxes are the linguistic and philosophical basis and pattern of *Othello*, in which nothing is what it seems to be, white is black, and generally things have two simultaneously true but contradictory aspects, like a bed, which represents birth and death, joy and grief. This feature creates ironies throughout the play on every level: plot, character, theme and language. Irony is one of the characteristics of tragedy, since it makes the outcome seem unfair and unnecessary, and therefore unacceptable, yet gives it an inevitability.

Many of the characters in the play are in themselves a paradox. Othello is an 'erring barbarian' and crusading Christian, 'bond-slave' and general, inarticulate orator, 'honourable murderer'. Although a rejected son-in-law, he is relied upon by the Senate (which includes his father-in-law) to protect Venice and is employed as an alien to kill other aliens — Moslems who are his own religious forebears. He is, as a personality, both confident and unsure of himself, trustful and doubtful, rational and superstitious. Desdemona is 'free of speech' with a rebellious streak, but also a pure and blushing maiden who knows her place and her duty to her lord, even to the point of forgiving him for killing her. Though representing the truth and the light, she dies 'like a liar gone to burning hell' (V.2.130). Iago seems to be the epitome of honesty, but he is not what he seems, as expressed in the paradoxical utterance 'I am not what I am' (I.1.66). He talks much of growth, when his interest is in destruction, of proof when he means implication. He is a contradiction in terms as a clever slave, a 'demi-devil', and an inhuman human. Cassio is thought worthy to be Othello's lieutenant — and later governor of Cyprus — but is a drunkard dismissed as unfit for service.

The main characters manage to achieve the exact opposite of that which they would wish to achieve: Brabantio loses the daughter he has tried to keep close to him; Cassio wants to impress his general and do well in his new job, but loses it in disgrace; Emilia loves her mistress enough to die for her, but is the cause of the missing handkerchief which condemns Desdemona to death, and she fails to win her husband's affection by stealing it; Cassio's visit to Desdemona compromises the person he would do anything not to harm; Othello wants to kill the two people who love him most, Desdemona and Cassio; he also wants to impress his Venetian bosses, and fails spectacularly. Some directors interpret Iago's intention to be to win Othello back for himself, the way things were before Desdemona and Cassio came on the scene, and instead he loses him for ever.

Virtues or vices?

With everyone he meets, Iago drags noble concepts downwards until they are totally demeaned: love, virtue, honesty, reputation. His obsession with sex and crude language turn love's gold into base metal. By winning for himself praise for being valiant and honest, he turns language and values upside down as well.

Iago's aim in the play is to turn fair into foul without being caught doing so: Cassio is made to perform as a drunkard; Roderigo loses his land and money and is made a gull; Desdemona is labelled a whore; Emilia is made a thief and an accessory to murder; Bianca is accused of conspiracy to murder. All of these characters have weaknesses which are not created by Iago, only noticed by him and exploited for his benefit and to their shame. He does not make anyone do anything by force; they walk freely into his spider's web. His main achievement is to get others — Cassio, Roderigo, Brabantio, Emilia — to see things the way he sees them, blackly; Othello borrows Iago's vision when he makes Iago his soul mate, and turns his wife into a strumpet, her maid into a bawd, his best friend into his sworn enemy.

Many of the characters have qualities that are essentially worthy but which are paradoxically able to be used by Iago as weapons against themselves or others. Desdemona's charitable mind and pity for others is a 'goodness' from which Iago can fashion a 'net' to 'enmesh them all' (II.3.352). Othello's desire for knowledge and objective 'ocular proof' so as not to fall into an error of judgement are what make it possible for Iago to abuse his eyes. Othello loves Desdemona because she is unconventional, but this can be later held against her. Cassio's good manners prevent him from refusing to drink a toast to the marriage and result in his getting drunk and injuring Montano.

There is an innate contradiction in the concept of innocence: it is a requirement for goodness, but it goes hand in hand with naïvety and involves a lack of protective knowledge of the ways of the world which leads to misjudgement and disaster. This paradox is inherent in the Fall: without experience one cannot protect oneself from those who wish to deprive us of innocence.

Two-sided events

There are major events in the play which can be seen as both honourable and dishonourable, foolish and wise, starting with the marriage, which is a joy for Desdemona but 'an evil' to her father. Othello thinks it a matter of male honour and Christian righteousness to kill Desdemona for committing adultery, though 'Thou shalt not kill' is one of the ten commandments; he breaks his marriage oath to Desdemona in order to keep his vengeance oath to Iago. His suicide is the ultimate example of a paradoxical act; self-slaughter is condemned by the Christian church, yet Othello is asserting his Christian credentials by enacting the slaying of a Turk, having just behaved like one himself by taking it upon himself to barbarically and unjustly execute an allegedly adulterous woman, without trial, something only permissible under Moslem law.

There are also many minor incidents or situations which could be termed para-doxical or ironic. The watch, i.e. the protectors of the peace, are the causers of the drunken street violence, the breaking of the curfew and the rousing of the populace. Emilia curses her own husband, and Brabantio curses himself, as well as his daughter. Roderigo's interest in Desdemona is sexual but he praises her 'blessed condition', and if she were actually available, he would not want her. Cassio consorts with a courtesan of whom he has a low opinion, whilst exalting the divinity of the female sex as personified by Desdemona. Othello thinks he finds evidence in his interrogation of Emilia in the 'brothel scene' that she is lying, but in fact she is telling the truth. He interprets all evidence of Desdemona's goodness as proof of her infidelity. He is provoked to kill her when she weeps for Cassio, when it was tears of pity which made him love her in the first place. She makes things worse for herself, Cassio and Othello by pleading so hard for Cassio's reinstatement, an altruistic act to reunite her husband and his best friend. By going to Othello's bed and losing her virginity, Desdemona becomes 'fallen' and shows evidence of a sexual appetite which makes it possible for Othello to imagine, and then suspect, that what she has done with him she could do with another man.

Desdemona dies whilst uttering a 'sublime falsehood', as the introduction to the *Penguin* edition calls it, confirming Othello's accusation that she is a liar though she is trying to save the life of her accuser. Iago is the main speaker and word manipulator in the play, but finally refuses to speak. It is painfully ironic to hear him being thanked, praised and rewarded for giving advice or information which is malicious. It is worrying that his amoral view of life, and of people as either flies or spiders, is an unacceptable one and yet proves to be accurate: the world of the play does consist of only fools and villains, and the punishment of virtue.

Love as war

War is inherently paradoxical, glorious and barbaric, and the play stresses that this is also true of love. Love is not under human control, and therefore cannot be rationally defined or measured, yet all the male characters in the play try to apply reason to explain it. Desdemona's genuine love for Othello cannot be shown in any way other than the ones she uses — obedience, loyalty, accompanying him to Cyprus — but these can also be seen as self-serving and suspicious. The handkerchief is a symbol of the paradox of love, in that Desdemona drops it in her sympathy for Othello's headache, but will then have it used as evidence of her not loving him.

Falling in love causes the betrayal of parents, evokes disgust from observers who do not approve the choice, and leads to jealousy, madness, murder, and many other sins and vices, yet it is vaunted as the highest, noblest emotion humans are capable of, is the basis of religion, and even Iago refers to the belief that love can make base men more noble (II.1.209–10). Love is easily confused with lust, infatuation, sex for money, and it can be easily debased from an abstract and altruistic state into a matter of 'a permission of the will' (I.3.331–32) and a crude bodily function. It is in the name of love that Othello kills Desdemona.

Nature erring from itself

One of the play's major paradoxes, as in the other major tragedies, is that nature itself is unnatural. Desdemona is the main representative of this in the play, being a 'fair devil' in three men's eyes, four counting Roderigo. According to her father and Iago — and, ironically, Othello in the end — her love for Othello proves that she is unnatural. As Iago says, 'she would never have loved the Moor' if she had been 'blessed', because he is perceived by the Venetians as an abnormality, and natural taste would incline her towards the younger, whiter and more handsome Cassio. Desdemona's unconventionality is also evidence of her unnaturalness. She goes against accepted codes of female behaviour in her society by being undutiful to her father, forward with suitors and outspoken in the Senate. At the time, women were in tune with nature if they were maidens or mothers (i.e. pure or fertile), but accused of being unnatural if they were spinsters, childless wives or whores (i.e. ugly and rejected by men, barren or promiscuous). Othello is a product of nature yet his skin colour renders him unnatural. Iago has inhuman qualities which cause him to be considered a devil, yet he too is man of woman born. All three of the main characters attract the word 'monstrous' (a word much used in the other major tragedies too), meaning not just horrible but an aberration of nature, which highlights the paradox that a monster can only exist in and be created by nature, yet is to be feared.

The effect of the play's use of paradox and irony on the audience is disconcerting. Our beliefs and securities are undermined and we are forced to shift our perceptions and re-evaluate our interpretations, which puts us in the same position as Othello. We, like him, suffer from not knowing what we really know and what can be trusted, or how to find information which can make us sure. To be in doubt is painful, and this is the state which paradox creates. If words and events are self-contradictory, then there is no truth to be had, the basis of human values and morals is brought into question, and we lose our confidence in being able to judge ourselves or our fellow humans.

Quotations

The best quotations to learn are those which can serve more than one purpose, i.e. which can be used to prove a theme or image usage as well as a point about a character or a dramatic effect. Think about which points each quotation below could be used to support in an examination or coursework essay.

Act I scene 1

- …by the faith of man,/I know my price, I am worth no worse a place — (Iago to Roderigo)
- …almost damned in a fair wife. (Iago about Cassio)
- …in following him, I follow but myself. (Iago about Othello)
- …I am not what I am. (Iago)
- …an old black ram/Is tupping your white ewe. (Iago to Brabantio)
- …your daughter and the Moor are now making the beast with two backs. (Iago to Brabantio)
- …an extravagant and wheeling stranger… (Roderigo about Othello)
- …belief of it oppresses me already. (Brabantio about the elopement)
- …I must show out a flag and sign of love. (Iago)

Act I scene 2

- …my services…/Shall out-tongue his complaints. (Othello about Brabantio)
- …my perfect soul/Shall manifest me rightly. (Othello)

- …the sooty bosom/Of such a thing as thou… (Brabantio to Othello)
- …bondslaves and pagans shall our statesmen be. (Brabantio)

Act I scene 3

- I saw Othello's visage in his mind. (Desdemona)
- A man he is of honesty and trust…(Othello about Iago)
- …your son-in-law is far more fair than black. (Duke to Brabantio)
- She has deceived her father, and may thee. (Brabantio to Othello)
- My life upon her faith! (Othello about Desdemona)
- We must obey the time.
- It is merely a lust of the blood and a permission of the will. (Iago about love)
- …a frail vow betwixt an erring barbarian and a super-subtle Venetian… (Iago about the marriage)
- There are many events in the womb of time, which will be delivered… (Iago)
- The Moor is of a free and open nature,/That thinks men honest that but seem to be so… (Iago)
- Hell and night/Must bring this monstrous birth to the world's light. (Iago)

Act II scene 1

- …the divine Desdemona…our great Captain's Captain. (Cassio to Iago)
- The great contention of the sea and skies/Parted our fellowship. (Cassio about himself and Othello)
- Nay it is true, or else I am a Turk… (Iago)
- …I do beguile/The thing I am by seeming otherwise. (Desdemona)
- …she'll find a white that shall her blackness fit. (Iago)
- With as little a web as this will I ensnare as great a fly as Cassio. (Iago)
- …it is too much of joy. (Othello about his reunion with Desdemona)
- …the thought whereof/Doth, like a poisonous mineral, gnaw my inwards… (Iago about jealousy)
- …knavery's plain face is never seen till used. (Iago)

Act II scene 3

- Are we turned Turks and to ourselves do that/Which heaven hath forbid the Ottomites? (Othello)
- Now, by heaven,/My blood begins my safer guides to rule… (Othello)
- Cassio, I love thee,/But nevermore be officer of mine. (Othello)
- I have lost the immortal part of myself, and what remains is bestial. (Cassio about reputation)
- …I'll pour this pestilence into his ear… (Iago about Othello)
- So will I turn her virtue into pitch,/And out of her own goodness make the net/That shall enmesh them all. (Iago about Desdemona)

Act III scene 3

- Perdition catch my soul/But I do love thee! And when I love thee not,/Chaos is come again (Othello about Desdemona)
- ...I'll see before I doubt; when I doubt, prove... (Othello)
- ...and when she seemed to shake, and fear your looks,/She loved them most... (Iago to Othello about Desdemona)
- I am bound to thee for ever. (Othello to Iago)
- ...I am abused, and my relief/Must be to loathe her. (Othello about Desdemona)
- Trifles light as air/Are to the jealous confirmations strong/As proofs of holy writ. (Iago)
- ...pride, pomp and circumstance of glorious war! (Othello)
- Villain, be sure thou prove my love a whore;/Be sure of it: give me the ocular proof... (Othello to Iago)
- Arise, black vengeance, from thy hollow cell! (Othello)
- I am your own for ever. (Iago to Othello)

Act III scene 4

- ...my noble Moor/Is true of mind... (Desdemona to Emilia)
- ...there's magic in the web of it. (Othello to Desdemona about the handkerchief)
- They are all but stomachs, and we all but food. (Emilia to Desdemona about men and women)
- It is a monster/Begot upon itself, born on itself. (Emilia on jealousy)

Act IV scene 1

- Thus credulous fools are caught... (Iago about Othello)
- A hornèd man's a monster and a beast. (Othello)

Act IV scene 2

- Heaven truly knows that thou art false as hell. (Othello to Desdemona)

Act IV scene 3

- ...I do think it is their husbands' faults/If wives do fall. (Emilia to Desdemona)

Act V scene 1

- ...he hath a daily beauty in his life/That makes me ugly... (Iago about Cassio)
- O damned Iago! O inhuman dog! (Roderigo)
- This is the night/That either makes me, or fordoes me quite. (Iago)

Act V scene 2

- Put out the light, and then put out the light... (Othello about Desdemona)
- Some bloody passion shakes your very frame... (Desdemona to Othello)

- She was too fond of her most filthy bargain. (Emilia about Desdemona to Othello)
- I will not charm my tongue; I am bound to speak... (Emilia)
- O cursèd, cursèd slave! Whip me, ye devils,/From the possession of this heavenly sight! (Othello about Desdemona's body)
- Where is this rash and most unfortunate man? (Lodovico about Othello)
- ...Othello, that wast once so good,/Fallen in the practice of a damnèd slave... (Lodovico)
- Demand me nothing; what you know, you know:/From this time forth I never will speak word. (Iago to Othello)
- ...one that loved not wisely, but too well... (Othello about himself)
- ...not easily jealous but, being wrought,/Perplexed in the extreme... (Othello about himself)

Critical voices

The following well-known critics' comments show changing attitudes over three centuries towards the play or its main characters. They could be useful to support your own opinion in an essay, or to provide evidence of alternative views.

- Why was not this called the tragedy of the handkerchief?...The tragical part of *Othello* is plainly none other than a bloody farce...If this be our end what boots it to be Vertuous?   Thomas Rymer, 1693

- ...the fiery openness of Othello, magnanimous, artless, and credulous, boundless in his confidence, ardent in his affection, inflexible in his resolution and obdurate in his revenge.   Dr Johnson, 1765

- ...the motive-hunting of motiveless malignity. [On Iago's soliloquy, Act I scene 3]   S. T. Coleridge, 1819

- The great moral lesson of the tragedy of *Othello* is that black and white blood cannot be intermingled in marriage without a gross outrage upon the law of Nature.   Quincy Adams, 1863

- His [Iago's] thwarted sense of superiority wants satisfaction...He is the spirit of denial of all romantic values.   A. C. Bradley, 1904

- Othello loves emotion for its own sake, luxuriates in it.   G. Wilson Knight, 1930

- Othello is too stupid to be regarded as a tragic hero.   F. R. Leavis, 1952

- A habit of self-approving self-dramatization is an essential element in Othello's make-up...the tragedy may fairly be said to be Othello's character in action...

  F. R. Leavis, 1952

- I have never read a more terrible exposure of human weakness than the last great speech of Othello.

  T. S. Eliot, 1953

- We are shown extremes with a kind of blank between...

  A. P. Rossiter, 1961

- ...the story of a melodramatic villain entrapping a credulous fool.

  K. Muir, 1972

- Othello's dreadful humiliation...at the hands of a plausible white thug.

  J. Suzman, 2006

Literary terms and concepts

The terms and concepts below have been selected for their relevance to writing about *Othello*. It will aid argument and expression to become familiar with them and to use them in your essays.

advocatus diaboli	literally the devil's lawyer, this means arguing a case one does not actually believe
ambiguity	capacity of words to have two simultaneous meanings in the same context, usually as a deliberate device for enriching the meaning of text
ambivalence	simultaneous coexistence of opposing feelings or attitudes
anagnorisis	moment of recognition by a character of an important truth
antithesis	contrast of ideas expressed by balancing words or phrases of opposite meaning
aside	remark spoken by a character in a play which is shared with the audience but unheard by characters on stage
blank verse	unrhymed **iambic pentameter**, the staple form of Shakespeare's plays
caesura	deliberate break in a line of verse, signified by punctuation
catharsis	Aristotle's claim that **tragedy** purges the audience through the feelings of pity and fear

climax	intense moment to which a series of actions has been leading
colloquial	informal language of speech
dénouement	unfolding of the final stages of a plot, when all is revealed
double entendre	expression with two meanings, one of which is indecent
dramatic irony	when the audience knows something a character does not
emotive	language which arouses an emotional response in the audience
end-stopped	pause created by punctuation at the end of a line of verse
enjamb(e)ment	run-on line of verse, usually to reflect meaning
eternal verities	fundamental and permanent truths of human existence
foot/feet	unit(s) of rhythm in verse
genre	type or form of writing
gothic	medieval art and literary genre depicting violence, death, horror, the supernatural and the macabre
hubris and Nemesis	over-reaching of a human who aspires to divine status, resulting in downfall, which is the punishment by Nemesis, goddess of retribution
hyperbole	deliberate exaggeration for effect, e.g. 'He's asked me a thousand times.'
iambic pentameter	five **feet** of iambs, i.e. alternating unstressed/stressed syllables
imagery	figurative descriptive language to build up atmosphere and develop themes in a literary work
in medias res	beginning a scene in the middle of an event or dialogue
irony	a discrepancy between the actual and implied meaning of language; or an amusing or cruel reversal of an outcome expected, intended or deserved
Machiavelli	in the early sixteenth century the Italian Niccolò Machiavelli, in his book *The Prince*, recommended ruthless self-interest and unethical methods to gain political power
metaphor	suppressed comparison, implied not stated, e.g. 'put out the light' ('light' referring to Desdemona)

micro/macrocosm	states in the individual mind, e.g. conflict, are reflected in larger contexts, e.g. civil war
oxymoron	phrase consisting of a contradiction in terms, e.g. 'fair devil'
paradox	self-contradictory statement or state of affairs
pathos	pity evoked by a situation of suffering and helplessness
peripeteia	sudden reversal of fortune
poetic justice	due allocation of reward and punishment for virtue and vice
pun	word(s) with double meaning for humorous or ironic effect
rhetoric	art of persuasion, using emotive language and syntax
rhyming couplet	a pair of adjacent rhyming lines
romance	story of love and heroism, deriving from medieval court life and fairy tale
seven deadly sins	according to the medieval Catholic church, the following sins led one straight to hell: pride, envy, gluttony, lechery, avarice, wrath, sloth
simile	comparison introduced by 'as' or 'like'
soliloquy	speech by character alone on stage
sources	stories which writers build into their own artistic creation
swan song	legend that mute swans sing only once, with haunting pathos, just before they die
symbol	object, person or event representing more than itself
theme	abstract idea or issue explored in a literary work
tragedy	drama concerning characters in high positions, with a fatal conclusion for the guilty and some of the innocent
the unities	three Aristotelian principles of dramatic composition whereby a play should consist of one related series of actions, occurring within one day, and taking place in one location
verse	language organised according to its rhythmical qualities into regular patterns of metre and set out in lines
willing suspension of disbelief	Coleridge's description of how an audience does not apply the normal rules of realism when watching drama

Questions & Answers

Othello

Essay questions, specimen plans and notes

Coursework essays

Below are some possible titles which would be appropriate for a coursework essay.

1 Explore how Shakespeare examines the themes of jealousy and deception in *Othello* the play and Othello the character. Compare your interpretation of *Othello* with those of other critics.

You should refer to the following:

- the characteristics of Shakespearean tragedy
- the key scenes which address the themes of jealousy and deception
- the dramatic impact these scenes would have on the audience
- how the original audience would have responded differently from a modern one
- how issues linked to jealousy and deception are revealed to the audience through characters, imagery and language
- how Othello contributes to the portrayal of these themes
- how themes of jealousy and deception have been commented on by various critics
- Othello as the tragic hero
- Othello's treatment of other characters
- Othello compared to other characters
- how Othello has been viewed by various critics
- your own view on how the themes of jealousy and deception are shown and developed in the play
- your own interpretation of *Othello*

(Source: AQA B, 2002)

Further questions

2 What interests you most about the play of *Othello*? Give a detailed analysis of the complexities and challenges of the play as far as a modern audience is concerned.

3 What contrasts are drawn in the play between the worlds of Venice and of Cyprus? How are these contrasts represented on stage?

4 Explore the character of Othello, showing how he develops through the play and saying how convincing you find him.

5 Explore the character of Iago, tracing and accounting for his behaviour throughout the play.

6 Choose any two characters who offer interesting points for comparison and contrast. Write a study of their roles in the play and your response to them as characters. (Suggestions: Desdemona and Emilia; Iago and Cassio; Cassio and Roderigo.)

7 How does Shakespeare portray women in the play? Examine the characterisation and function of the female characters.

8 Does Shakespeare succeed in individualising the minor characters? Consider four or five examples to support your answer.

9 Write about the use of imagery in *Othello* and its contribution to the overall effect of the play.

10 What have you gained in your knowledge of Shakespeare and his period by your study of this play and its critics?

Exam essays

The exemplar essay questions which follow can be used for planning practice and/or full essay writing within the time limit, with or without the text. Many have been previously set by different exam boards for various specifications. In each of the three sections there are some essay titles with suggestions for ideas to include in a plan, and some with examiners' notes and guidance on how to approach the question. Two questions are provided with sample student answers. Remember to talk about the play and the audience, not the book and the reader, and try to visualise how it would appear on stage and how it would sound; the drama and the poetry are essential elements of the written text you are being asked to respond to. Here are the questions to address when analysing drama text passages:

- Is it all verse, all prose, or a mixture?
- Is it primarily looking forward to something which is to come, or looking backwards to explain or reinforce a previous event?
- Are there any entrances or exits, and what effect do they have if so?
- Look at stage directions. What are the visual effects of the position of characters, props and the actions being performed?
- Comment on the imagery and relate it to other usages and its link with themes.
- Is there a dominant or silent presence or one who is given relatively few lines?
- Is there any irony or dramatic irony? Who knows what at this stage?
- Where is the audience's sympathy, and why?
- Is the passage similar to or a contrast to another episode?
- How does the language and its tone reveal character, and how does it affect the audience's feelings about something or someone?
- How does the scene further the plot and themes? Why is it there?

Whole-text questions: open text

Note: some of the questions in this section could be suitable as closed-text questions.

1 'It is essential to the development of the play's tragic situation that Othello, Iago and Cassio are soldiers.' How far do you agree with this view? In your answer you should discuss characters and motives, narrative development and setting. You should also show an awareness of Elizabethan attitudes to gender and honour, as well as an awareness of Shakespearean tragedy.

AO1 Lucid expression in a relevant and well-organised answer.

AO3 Perceptive and detailed insight into the varying soldier characters of the play, their military status and accompanying attitudes – to honour, to women, to reputation, for example; and sensitivity to Shakespeare's handling of the military setting and development of the narrative arising from the motivation of the soldiers in defence of their honour.

AO4 Mature and thoughtful judgement of the critical view expressed, weighing how far it can be accepted and why – the word 'essential' may be challenged; informed by an awareness of differing points of view.

AO5i Good understanding of Elizabethan attitudes to cuckoldry, military and personal honour and the structure of Shakespearean tragedy.

(Source: Top band descriptors, OCR 2000 specimen materials)

Further questions

2 How far do you agree that Iago's dramatic persona appeals to different audiences in different ways?

3 'Both Othello's jealousy itself and the speed with which it develops are absurd.' Discuss the validity of this view of *Othello*.

4 Iago comments about Cassio that:

> He hath a person and a smooth dispose
>
> To be suspected: framed to make women false (Act I scene 3)

and, later:

> That Cassio loves her, I do well believe it;
>
> That she loves him 'tis apt and of great credit (Act II scene 1).

How do you see the relationship between Cassio and Desdemona? What is its importance in the play?

5 Desdemona and Emilia are companions and friends, yet they are different in character. Explore the differences between them. Where do your sympathies lie when you see or read the play?

6
> He has a daily beauty in his life
>
> That makes me ugly (V.1.19–20)

Iago says of Cassio. What exactly is he saying about Cassio and himself?

7 'Jealousy in the play is not confined to Othello.' Where else is it important?

8 Describe and interpret the roles of the three women in *Othello*.

9 'Men are the sport of circumstances when/Circumstances seem the sport of men.' (Lord Byron). How far is it true that Iago becomes trapped by his own subtlety?

10 Wilson Knight said 'Othello loves emotion for its own sake, luxuriates in it.' Do you think there is any truth in this accusation?

11 'The enduring interest of the play is its treatment of race and the outsider.' Do you agree?

12 This is 'the story of a man who went into a house', i.e. who was unfit for domesticity. Do you believe that this has any relevance to the outcome of the play?

13 'Othello was not jealous, he was trustful.' Examine Dostoyevsky's view of Othello's weakness.

14 Leavis said 'the tragedy may fairly be said to be Othello's character in action'. Say whether or not you agree with this view of Othello and the play.

15 How does Shakespeare convey the strengths and weaknesses of Othello's character?

16 'The great failing of *Othello* is that Desdemona and Emilia are too weak and easily deceived to be convincing.' How far do you agree with this criticism of the play?

Whole-text questions: closed text

Note: some of the questions in this section could be suitable as open-text questions.

1 Leavis claimed that 'A habit of self-approving self-dramatization is an essential element in Othello's make-up.' Do you agree with this description of Othello's character?

Possible ideas to include in a plan

- Moor a common stage figure of the time, stereotypically represented as larger than life with huge appetites and uncontrolled emotions
- tragic hero has flaw or makes an error of judgement; Othello's weakness is his tendency to excess, exaggeration and showing-off
- has general's belief in a just cause, putting him in the right and giving him an authority to chastise others
- an outsider not confident in 'super-subtle Venetian' world, and may be over-compensating
- from first meeting Othello appears arrogant and without interest in the viewpoint of others
- Roderigo describes him as an 'extravagant' 'stranger'
- a story-teller dramatises and exaggerates, and this is how Othello has won people's admiration and pity (e.g. Brabantio and Desdemona)
- lives life as a fiction; has over-active imagination which makes him vulnerable to Iago's conjuring of gross pictures of Desdemona's sexual activity with Cassio
- rages and epileptic fit a form of dramatic attention-seeking
- veers between absolute trust and gullibility of the 'credulous fool', without a middle way
- allows Iago to become his director because he is too engrossed in acting; communes with himself and puts on performances for others

- deeply egocentric; use of 'I' or his own name dominant throughout
- Eliot thought his final speech was a way of comforting himself, a return to demanding attention and applause

Further questions

2 Do you think Iago has any valid reasons for treating Othello in the way he does? Comment on the evidence for Iago's motives, your own views of Iago's character and actions, and the relevance of contemporary attitudes to class, rank and women.

3 A critic has claimed that there is a 'hollowness at the centre' of *Othello*. What do you think this means, and do you agree?

4 'The play is a beautifully contrived arrangement of patterns.' Discuss some of the patterns and comment on their effect.

5 Bradley says of Iago, 'He is the spirit of denial of all romantic values.' Is this how you see Iago?

6 Charles Lamb described *Othello* as the story of 'a consummate villain entrapping a noble nature into toils against which no discernment was available'. Do you agree that Othello could not have protected himself from Iago and prevented himself from falling into his trap?

7 How successful is Shakespeare in creating (i) exotic atmosphere and (ii) the background of war, and to what dramatic use does he put them?

8 How far do you agree with the Leavis view that 'Othello is too stupid to be regarded as a tragic hero'?

9 Othello claims that his downfall was caused by loving 'not wisely, but too well'. What does he mean? Do you agree with him?

10 'The main theme of *Othello* is not jealousy but honour.' Explore this claim.

11 '*Othello* is the tale of a gullible hero deceived by a melodramatic villain.' Is this an adequate description of the play?

12 *Othello* has been described as 'much ado about a handkerchief'. Is this a fair comment?

13 'The real tragedy of the play is that Othello proves that the world really is as Iago sees it.' Explain this claim and say whether you agree with it.

14 'The action of *Othello* is no less than the Fall of Man, the failure of humanity.' Examine and evaluate this proposition.

15 Desdemona has often been seen only as the innocent victim of malice. Do you agree with this judgement of her?

16 '*Othello* is a tragedy without meaning and that is the ultimate horror of it.' What support can you find in the play for this opinion?

Passage-based essay questions

The question you choose may direct you to a prescribed passage or ask you to select your own. Either way you will need to show your knowledge of the whole play as well as your response to and analysis of a particular sequence. Careful selection of passages is crucial to ensure the relevance and success of the essay; the passages you like or are most familiar with are not necessarily the most appropriate for a particular title. Do not waste time paraphrasing what happens in the scene or the content of the speech or dialogue; just give a quick summary of its setting and context, along the lines of who is present and why, what has just happened, what will follow, and what its dramatic purpose is.

Examiners advise that reference to the rest of the work should be as much as 60% of the essay even for a passage-based question. Focus closely on the passage(s) but also relate the content and/or language to elsewhere in the text, backwards and forwards, and link your comments to the overall themes and/or structure of the play. Include references to character, event, theme and language, and ask how the extract modifies or adds to our understanding so far, and how typical it is of the work as a whole. Think about reader/audience reaction, using your own as the basis for your response.

Passage-based questions: prescribed

1 **Remind yourself of the final meeting and dialogue between Othello and Desdemona in the last scene of the play, from 'Othello: It is the cause' to 'Othello: Ay, and for that thou diest' (V.2.1–41). What might the thoughts and feelings of an audience be as they watch this sequence? You should show an awareness of the characteristics of dramatic climax and Shakespearean tragedy. Suggest how audience reactions may differ to it.**

AO1 Lucid expression in a relevant and well-organised answer.

AO3 Perceptive and detailed insight into the complex characterisation of Othello by examination of the imagery he uses and his tortured ambivalence of tone: the contrast of the soliloquy and the tense dialogue; Desdemona's innocent and pitiful responses and their contributions to the tragic, suspenseful atmosphere of the scene.

AO4 Mature and thoughtful judgement of the qualities of the scene at this point; it is close to the murder of Desdemona and response could be intense, informed by an awareness that some audiences/readers might find either Othello or Desdemona unsympathetic characters (for different reasons), whilst others might see them both as tragic victims.

AO5i Good understanding of the tragic structure of the play and the impending climax; sensitivity to the development of the tragic hero within this structure.

(Source: top band descriptors, OCR 2000 specimen materials)

2 **Look again at Act II scene 3. By a careful examination of this scene consider the importance of Shakespeare's presentation of the military context in which the action is set to your understanding of the play as a whole.**

AO1   Candidates will need to offer some definition of the 'military context' of the play: some will focus on the question of rank and the responsibilities attaching to it, particularly in times of war; others will consider the attitudes and approaches to life a military life inculcates and expects.

AO2ii The question requires candidates to consider the scene in the context of the play as a whole; the quality of comparison they offer with the rest of the play will depend on the range of different aspects of the military context which they identify in the prescribed scene, from the respective positions of Othello, Cassio and Iago, to the sense of measure which informs their behaviour.

AO3   The key word here is 'presentation'; at the bottom end answers are likely to focus on action and characterisation, while at the top they are likely to consider the importance of structure and the parallels and resonances this sets up.

AO4   The question presents candidates with an angle on the text to which to respond; quality of argument will be a significant discriminator here, with some candidates simply asserting the importance of the military context, while others assess its relative importance, possibly suggesting that other elements are more vital to an understanding of the play as a whole.

AO5ii The question invites direct consideration of the importance of the military context and candidates are likely also to consider the importance of the racial dimension; what will distinguish them here will be the extent to which they consider the influence of the external Elizabethan military, political and social context on the play, and the impact of their own historical, cultural, social and racial perspective on their response to the play.

(Source: Edexcel specimen mark scheme, January 2000)

3 **Look again at Act V scene 2, from Othello's entrance until the death of Desdemona. Dr Johnson, in the eighteenth century, found this scene so moving as to be unendurable. What is your response to this part of the scene? How far do you sympathise with Dr Johnson?**

AO1   Interpretation of the phrase 'so moving as to be unendurable' will be key here, with some candidates taking it to mean no more than poignant while others will register its full force, conscious of its implication that the scene is at the absolute limit of what is bearable to witness.

AO2ii To satisfy this AO candidates will need to identify the play as a tragedy: some candidates may do no more than this, while others will set the scene in the context of the play as a whole and consider the part played by structure in generating emotion in the audience.

AO3   Reward for answers against this AO will depend on the quality of textual analysis offered, likely to range from observation of the contrast between Othello's opening speech and his actions thereafter, to detailed consideration of the characters' speeches, noting the changes in the style and language of Othello's in contrast to the essential steadiness of Desdemona's, and examining the internal structure of the scene, with its changes of pace, its double climax, and registering also the intense dramatic irony which runs through the scene.

AO4   The question requires candidates to give their own response and to consider Johnson's: some candidates are likely simply to say whether or not they personally find the scene moving, while others will respond to the full force of Johnson's comment, assess its validity, and perhaps suggest alternative responses.

AO5ii The question introduces the idea of historical perspective; what will distinguish candidates is how they pursue this: their answers are likely to range from a simple contrasting of modern and earlier attitudes, to an evaluation of the significance of context in literary study, with candidates likely to point to the fact that Johnson's criticism has contributed to a definition of tragedy which underpins modern thinking.

(Source: top band descriptors, OCR 2000 specimen materials)

Further questions

4 Look again at the end of the play, from the entrance of Montano, Gratiano and Iago (V.2.167). In what ways do you find this an effective ending to a tragedy?

5 Look at Act III scene 3, lines 29–92. Comment on the significance of this extract to the language of the play, its characterisation and the development of the plot.

6 Remind yourself of the events of Act I. How do they prepare the audience for what is to follow? Look at themes, images, language, character and relationships.

7 Look again at the Willow Scene (Act IV scene 3) between Desdemona and Emilia. A critic has described it as 'the emotional peak of the evening'. What do you think he is referring to? What do the setting and the song add to the themes, characterisation and atmosphere of the play?

8 'In *Othello* Shakespeare explores the nature of social prejudice.' How far does your reading of the play support this view? You should use as a starting point for your answer a close examination of Act I scene 2 (from 'Othello: Holla, stand there') to Act I scene 3 (down to 'Brabantio: God bu'y! I have done').

9 Turn to Act I scene 3 and remind yourself of the section that begins with Othello's line 'The tyrant custom, most grave senators' (line 227) and ends with the exit of Desdemona and Othello. Bearing in mind your knowledge of the whole play, what do you find of dramatic interest and significance in this extract?

10 Look at the first 100 lines of Act IV scene 1 (up to the stage direction 'Enter Cassio'). What is their dramatic impact upon an audience? How do they reveal Iago's total command at this stage of the play?

11 In Act III scene 3 (after 'Exeunt Desdemona and Emilia'), Othello says (lines 90–92):

> Excellent wretch, perdition catch my soul,
> But I do love thee, and when I love thee not,
> Chaos is come again.

Iago speaks and interrupts Othello's thinking. From then until his exit (line 255), how does Iago manage to undermine Othello's love for Desdemona? What is dramatic in this part of the scene?

12 Turn to Act IV scene 2 and remind yourself of the section that begins immediately after the entry of Iago and Emilia, with Iago's line: 'What is your pleasure, madam? How is't with you?' The section ends with the exit of Desdemona and Emilia some 65 lines later. What dramatic techniques does Shakespeare employ here, and what effects might these have on an audience?

13 'I have never read a more terrible exposure of human weakness than the last great speech of Othello', said T. S. Eliot. Analyse the speech and say whether you agree.

14 Read Act III scene 4 from line 51 ('I have a salt and sorry rheum') to Othello's exit (line 95). In what ways does this dialogue develop your response to Othello in the play as a whole? Look closely at language and tone, and comment on the issues relevant to married relationships and tensions between different cultures.

Passage-based questions: selected

1 Select and analyse a sequence which reveals Othello's attitude towards female sexuality.

Possible ideas to include in a plan

- men expected to control women's sexuality
- Othello's view of women is 'turned' by Iago
- Othello starts with excessively idealised language of religion and romantic love to and about Desdemona (to Senate in Act II scene 1 and on his arrival in Cyprus)
- by contrast his speeches in the sequence IV.2.1–93 – the 'brothel scene' – are a diatribe against women as sexual beings
- he makes direct accusations of Desdemona's fornication to both Emilia and Desdemona, accusing the former of complicity and being a bawd for profit
- relevant themes are seeming, doubt, dishonesty, corruption of money
- he does not accept the truthful answers from either woman because he assumes they are lying, self-fulfilling his prejudiced expectation, and that women gang up against men, ironically untrue in this case
- he contrasts women's false appearance of piety in kneeling and praying with the 'subtle whore' and 'cunning whore' he thinks they really are beneath the surface (Iago's diction and opinion)
- he treats both women as servants and with equal contempt, showing that once a woman's reputation has been blackened (by sexual slander) she falls from both her pedestal and her social position
- he sends both women away rather than accord them the status of human beings capable of rational conversation
- his speech (lines 46–63) is really a soliloquy and reveals his terror at women's power

to dishonour men and his disgust at unlicensed female sexual activity (meaning not governed by a single male)

- his wrath takes the form of a misogynistic tirade (lines 70–79); his language revolves around heaven and hell, giving women the responsibility not only for men's honour but for their salvation or perdition
- women are chaste angels or foul strumpets, the two extreme and only possibilities; both fictional constructs by men; women trapped and defenceless
- he feels as cheated in his having married her as Cassio would in being tricked into marrying Bianca
- he believes it would be a noble cause to dispose of her to protect men

Further questions

2   One not easily jealous, but being wrought
     Perplex'd in the extreme.
Select and analyse two passages which show Shakespeare's use of extremes and excess in *Othello*.

3 To what extent do you agree that in *Othello* Shakespeare presents 'women as victims of men'? You should base your answer on a close examination of two or more appropriate sequences of your choice.

4 Clemen described Othello as a 'character endowed with a rich imagination'. Refer to two or three passages which reveal Othello's 'rich imagination' and discuss its significance to the play as a whole.

5 Choose a particular scene or self-contained section of the play and give a full analysis of it, commenting on what it reveals about characters and themes; its dramatic effect; its use of language; and why you find it interesting.

Sample essays

Below are two sample essays of different types written by different students. Both of them have been assessed as falling within the top band. You can judge them against the Assessment Objectives for this text for your exam board and decide on the mark you think each deserves and why. You will also be able to see ways in which each could be improved in terms of content, style and accuracy.

Sample essay 1

Reread Act V scene 2 from line 280 to the end. In what ways do you find this an effective ending to the play as a tragedy?

In your answer you should:
- look closely at the language and tone that the characters use here

- explain your own views of how Shakespeare brings the play to an end
- comment on the place of relevant issues such as tragedy and honour

I think that this is an extremely effective ending to the play as a tragedy. To explain this I will first reveal how the language and the tone of the characters help to make it a good ending. It is Othello's language and tone which really establishes a sombre mood. After everything that has happened the audience have been willing Othello to see through Iago, who is ironically referred to as 'honest' throughout the play. Now that Othello knows how Iago has manipulated him, he returns to his majestic noble self comparing himself to a 'circumcised dog' and 'base indian'. The audience at this point will feel extreme sympathy for Othello, and will feel all the emotions of pity and terror that are associated with the tragedy genre.

Othello tells Lodovico that 'must you speak/Of one that loved not wisely but too well; Of one, not easily jealous but, being wrought,/Perplexed in the extreme'. In this statement Othello's language is richly poetic, and sees the return to Othello's dignified idiom. Here Othello has become a sad, wiser man and he is revealing a poetic insight into this life, and his faults. This is often the case in the genre of tragedy as, for example, King Lear's dying thoughts are for his daughter Cordelia, and in *Hamlet*, the hero also lets the audience into his poetic language. This is an effective ending because the noble hero, however stupid he may have been, can be forgiven by the audience, and they can feel love and pity for him.

The tone of this ending is quite sombre and terrifying in places, because the audience does not know what is going to happen next. The tone changes throughout the scene: at first Othello speaks in a harsh tone – 'O thou pernicious caitiff', but then his tone is more soft and reflective – 'Soft you, a word or two before you go.' This is important, I think because it emphasises a slowing-down of pace which is contradictory to the violence that has gone on before. This prepares the audience for the end of the play, which I think is extremely effective. A critic in the eighteenth century, Dr Johnson, said that he admired the construction and structure of the play, and I agree with him because the structure prepares the audience for the end.

Othello's honour and pride are conveyed well throughout the play. Othello's poetic language, which is full of military images, establishes Othello as a great military man, 'I have done the state some service'. His reputation and honour are very important to him, and this would have been recognised as important by an audience of Shakespeare's time. Perhaps Othello thought that Desdemona was a prize for his military victories, which is why he states 'Othello's occupation gone' when he thinks Desdemona has been unfaithful. Othello reinforces his honour and pride when he kills himself. He is no longer the brutal jealous man who was infected by Iago's bestial imagery – 'goats and monkeys' – but he is dignified, honourable as well as showing pride. An audience of Shakespeare's time would have recognised and appreciated this.

Shakespeare has effectively brought the tragedy to a finish, I think because he shows the audience how a 'truly noble hero, who does not belong to our world' (as A. C. Bradley once described Othello) can give in to a strong and powerful emotion such as jealousy, and can be manipulated by a 'villainous knave' such as Iago. Yet he is noble and strong enough to take his own life when he discovers the truth. I think it is also an effective ending because it can change the contempt that an audience of Shakespeare's time would have had for foreigners. By revealing Othello as majestic, noble and mythical: 'Drop tears as fast as the Arabian trees/their med'cinable gum', Shakespeare is trying to change the audience's racist views, and I think the ending is sufficient in doing this.

In most tragedy genres, nature participates in the hero's fall, but in Othello there is no great storm scene such as in King Lear or the sun failing to rise in Macbeth. There is however a great purpose in using the internal character study instead of moving from the microcosm to the macrocosm (reverberations leading to the collapse of the state in other tragedies). This ensures that the audience really knows the characters well, because attention has been focused in on them, which is why the problems between the Venetians and Turkish people resolved quickly. This is also effective in the ending because it is through the language of the characters that the events are concluded in the best possible way.

(Reproduced by kind permission of OCR)

Sample essay 2

'The great failing of *Othello* is that Desdemona and Emilia are too weak and easily deceived to be convincing.' How far do you agree with this criticism of the play?

In your answer you should:
- set out clearly the arguments for and against this claim
- explain your own views about Shakespeare's presentation of Desdemona and Emilia
- comment on the place of relevant issues such as the role of women in the play

The criticism that Desdemona and Emilia are too weak and easily deceived is a good argument to be considered. There are many arguments for and against this claim, but I think that there are more arguments against this claim, which I will now outline. Emilia is not a weak character, and I think she represents how the female voice should be heard. Emilia not only defends herself but her sex when Iago derides women: 'You shall not write my praise'. She is also sharp witted – 'is this man not jealous?' and has such strength that she says what she thinks – 'I will not charm my tongue I am bound to speak'. Emilia also becomes her mistress' defender, she is a strong character as well as convincing.

Her only flaw is that she did not understand her husband Iago, and was deceived by him. Even though this does happen, she had suspicions about him all along which is why she repeats 'my husband' several times when Othello tells her about him because she is thinking her doubts and suspicions through. If Emilia was 'weak' then she would not have the ability to bring about the downfall of the clever and extremely convincing Iago. She begins the process which leads to Iago's undoing – showing her intelligence as well as her strength.

I think that Desdemona is represented very differently from Emilia, as she is weaker than Emilia, but she is still a very strong convincing character. Brabantio says she was a 'maiden never bold of spirit so quiet and still that her motion blushed at herself'. Yet when she enters, she contradicts everything that has been said about her because she is perceptive – 'I do perceive a divided duty' – and shows an ability to sort out problems – 'I am hitherto your daughter but here is my husband'. She is so strong that she has asserted her independence from a male patriarchy. This was an extremely brave thing to do because women had little power, and had to do what their 'men' relationships told them to do. Thus Desdemona is not only strong but she is responsible, sensitive 'a child to chiding' and is extremely sympathetic (for example Othello's headache).

I think Shakespeare has presented Desdemona as such an innocent character that she does not fully understand the depth of Othello's jealous emotions. She totally misinterprets the handkerchief case, and even when Othello was getting more and more angry, she kept talking about Cassio which suggested she had feelings for him. She has such love and commitment for Othello, she wants to live with him in every sense and can't bear to be parted from him – 'the rites for which I love him are bereft me, let me go with him'. Yet her innocence and purity means she is blinded by her love for him, and does not truly understand him or the situation.

After examining the ideas for and against this argument I strongly disagree with the statement because neither Emilia or Desdemona are weak. I think Shakespeare has presented the strength of womanhood. He has presented a wide viewpoint on women. Emilia who is a pragmatic about relationships – 'they are all but stomacks and we all but food' and Desdemona who is idealistic – 'tell me Emilia that there be wifes that do abuse their husbands in such gross kind'. Both characters are trying to understand men in the world they live in. Iago's misogyny triumphs, however, as even when Emilia and Desdemona are alone talking, the topic is men and how to interpret them.

Desdemona is presented as such a strong character that even when Othello hits her she says 'I have not deserved this' but respects Othello's authority over her, and does not put up a fight when Othello kills her. She will even damn herself by lying for Othello – 'Nobody, I farewell' shows how she won't tell Emilia that Othello killed her. As Marilyn French (a twentieth-century critic) said, 'Desdemona is a symbol of female passivity' and I strongly agree with this.

The role of women in *Othello* is to show how women can be persecuted and vindicted [sic] by men. I think Shakespeare uses Desdemona and Emilia in *Othello* to represent how the strength of women in that society is increasing, giving inspiration and advice to the Shakespearean audience. In some cases I think Desdemona and Emilia are deceived, but they are wonderfully strong characters and their deaths represent their nobility. This is why I do not agree with this statement.

(Reproduced by kind permission of OCR)

Further study

Books

Bayley, J. (1981) *Shakespeare and Tragedy*, Routledge

Bradley, A. C. (1904) *Shakespearean Tragedy*, Routledge

Clemen, W. (1951) *The Development of Shakespeare's Imagery*, Harvard University Press

Harbage, A. (ed.) (1964) *Shakespeare: The Tragedies*, Prentice-Hall

Hawkes, T. (ed.) (1969) *Coleridge on Shakespeare*, Penguin Shakespeare Library

Heilman, R. B. (1956) *Magic in the Web: Action and Language in Othello*, Greenwood Press

Honigmann, E. A. J. (1976) *Shakespeare: Seven Tragedies*, Macmillan

Honigmann, E. A. J. (1989) *Myriad-Minded Shakespeare*, Macmillan

Kermode, F. (2000) *Shakespeare's Language*, Allen Lane

Leech, C. (1969) *Tragedy*, the *Critical Idiom* series, general editor John D. Jump, Routledge

Lerner, L. (ed.) (1963) *Shakespeare's Tragedies*, Penguin

Muir, K. (1972) *Shakespeare's Tragic Sequence*, Hutchinson University Library

Neely, C. T. (1985) *Broken Nuptials in Shakespeare's Plays*, University of Illinois Press

Rosenberg, M. (1961) *The Masks of Othello*, University of Delaware Press

Rossiter, A. P. (1961) *Angel with Horns: 15 Lectures on Shakespeare*, Longman

Spurgeon, C. F. E. (1935) *Shakespeare's Imagery and What It Tells Us*, Cambridge University Press

Wain, J (ed.) (1971) *Othello: A Casebook*, Macmillan

Wilson Knight, G. (1930) *The Wheel of Fire*, Routledge

Films

Othello has proved a popular subject for film-makers from the birth of the industry. No fewer than four silent black-and-white versions were made between 1907 and 1922, and at least another 15 films have been made since then. Particularly memorable productions include:

1952: directed by Orson Welles, who also took the part of Othello.

1965: directed by Stuart Burge, John Dexter's stage production with Laurence Olivier as Othello.

1981: BBC Shakespeare, directed by Jonathan Miller, with Anthony Hopkins as Othello and Bob Hoskins as Iago, with a cockney accent.

1986: directed by Franco Zeffirelli, Verdi's opera of *Otello*, with Placido Domingo.

1987: South African version directed by Janet Suzman during apartheid.

1989: American version directed by Ted Lange.

1995: Oliver Parker's film with Kenneth Branagh as Iago and Laurence Fishburne, the first big-screen black Othello.

1995: Royal Shakespeare Company's 1989 production directed by Trevor Nunn, with Willard White as Othello and Iago played by Ian McKellen as a working-class outsider with a northern accent.

2001: modern television drama directed by Geoffrey Sax set in the Metropolitan police force.

Internet

There are now a vast number of sites on the internet with useful material on Shakespeare and *Othello*. A Google search for 'Othello' returns 326,000 pages, although not all are useful and a substantial number refer to a proprietary game of the same name.

- **http://shakespeare.palomar.edu/** *Mr William Shakespeare and the Internet* is one of the best general Shakespeare sites. It includes general information and an extensive set of links to other sites, many of which include the full text of some or all of the plays, listed at **http://shakespeare.palomar.edu/works.htm** Most of these have some form of search engine which allows the text to be searched for words or phrases.
- **http://www.eamesharlan.org/tptt/** This site includes a word count, and line-count by character, for each play.

In addition to *Othello* sections in or referred to in the sites above, there are a number of individual sites worthy of note:

- **http://www.sparknotes.com/shakespeare/othello/** is a good introductory site, with the full text, notes and search engine
- **http://absoluteshakespeare.com/guides/othello/othello.htm** includes Coleridge's famous essay on the play
- **http://www.croftstudycentre.freeserve.co.uk/othello.htm** has a useful summary and some critical comments
- **http://www.mcauley.acu.edu.au/staff/simonr/othello.htm** is a useful site
- **http://www.unibas.ch/shine/linkstragothellowf.html** lists resources
- **http://web.uvic.ca/shakespeare/Annex/DraftTxt/Oth/index.htm** has texts of the Quarto and Folio accessible by scene or by page
- **http://www.shakespeare-online.com/essays/othelloessays.asp** contains a good collection of essays on *Othello*

Individual essays on *Othello*, of varying quality, include:

- **http://www.sirbacon.org/othello.htm**
- **http://www.geocities.com/Wellesley/7261/gripe5.html** (on Moors)

- http://www.calvin.edu/academic/engl/346/proj2/team1/crtintp.htm (critical interpretations of race in *Othello* over the centuries)

Pictures of historical Othellos may be found at:
- http://www.colby.edu/personal/l/leosborn/othello.html
- http://www.utdallas.edu/~kmarshal/Shakespeare/oth_page1.htm

Other useful websites include:
- http://www.clicknotes.com/othello/Osource.html includes the text of Cinthio's tale upon which Othello is based
- http://www.shakespeares-globe.org/ is the official website of the reconstructed Globe Theatre
- http://www.rdg.ac.uk/globe/ provides details of the original Globe
- http://www.shakespeare.org.uk is the site of the Shakespeare Birthplace Trust